Part of the Ilkley Tithe Map, 1847.

ILKLEY

The History of a
Wharfedale Town

Looking down to White Wells and the town below.

ILKLEY
The History of a Wharfedale Town

Rhona Finlayson

PHILLIMORE

2009

Published by
PHILLIMORE & CO. LTD
Chichester, West Sussex, England
www.phillimore.co.uk
www.thehistorypress.co.uk

ISBN 978-1-86077-567-3

Printed and bound in Great Britain

Contents

List of Illustrations

Acknowledgements

The author would like to thank all those who have helped to bring this book to press. The Local Studies Library at Ilkley was vital resource with special thanks due in particular to Caroline Brown for all her help. Many thanks are given to Bradford Library Service for giving permission to reproduce images from their Shuttleworth Collection here and to Bradford Museums, Manor House Museum and Gavin Edwards for giving permission to use images of Roman tomb stones. The helpfulness of the staff at West Yorkshire Archives was greatly appreciated as was their permission to reproduce images of specific documents in their keeping. West Yorkshire Archaeological Service is thanked for allowed the use of their artwork (their artist's impression of the Roman fort) as are Keith Boughey and Ed Vickerman who generously allowed me to use some of the images of carved rocks from their extensive and knowledgeable work on the subject. I am very thankful to Mr Paul Anning for kindly allowing permission to use copies of photographs taken by his father. I thank All Saints Church for giving permission to take photographs. Postcards used in illustration came from the author's collection but grateful thanks to J. Salmon Ltd for allowing reproduction of their vintage postcard of Ilkley White Wells; to the National Archives for allowing postcards by Walter Scott to be reproduced here; and to St Andrews University Photograph Archive who hold postcards by Valentine. Grateful thanks also to the National Library of Australia for allowing reproduction of the sketch by William Henty. Finally my particular thanks go to Laurence Truman for his unfailing assistance in his scrutiny of the text and for his permission to reproduce some of his photographs.

Illustration Acknowledgements

Anning (1954), 101, 123, 134, 147; K. Boughey and E. Vickerman, 5, 8, 11 (inset), 14; Bradford Library Collections, 24, 34, 39, 42-6, 48-9, 57, 59, 60-4, 67-73, 75-6, 78-80, 85-100, 104, 106-8, 111, 114, 118, 120-2, 125-6, 128-130, 135-43, 148: Bradford Museums, Galleries & Heritage, 22-3; Rhona Finlayson, 1-4, 6-7, 9-13, 15-17, 19, 21, 25-30, 33, 35-7, 50-5, 58, 77, 115, 120; Al Leith, 149; National Library of Australia, 41, front cover; Ordnance Survey map (1906), 65, 74, 119, rear endpaper; J. Prudhoe (West Yorkshire Archaeological Service), 20; Walter Scott, 55-6, 124; J. Solomon Ltd, 145; Laurence Truman, 18, 31-2, 47; Valantine, 127, 146; West Yorkshire Archive Service, 38, 40, 81-4, front endpaper, back cover.

One

PREHISTORIC LIFE ON ILKLEY MOORLAND

The Wharfe valley was formed by the combined forces of glacial ice and subsequent river action and this has given the valley at Ilkley distinctly different forms. The north side of the valley, although steep in places, has wide gentle slopes; the south side, on which Ilkley is located, is overshadowed by a steeply terraced valley rising to 400 metres above sea level, with dramatic rock outcrops and deeply incised tributary valleys created by the scouring effect of ice on the underlying millstone grit and the erosive effect of rainfall. As it retreated the glacier left behind moraines of clay and limestone, creating areas of rough hummocky ground and strewing boulder erratics around. This striking landscape, which has been changed over time by natural forces and human activities, provides a dramatic landscape against which the town of Ilkley has developed and has proved a strong influence on the town itself.

Ilkley and the other populous towns and villages in the Wharfe valley lie along the lower slopes, close to the river, but in prehistoric times it was the higher ground that was populated. These forested and moorland slopes to each side of the river Wharfe have been inhabited since the first Mesolithic hunter-gatherers followed the retreating glacial ice and settled here approximately 11,000 years ago. The rich and extensive evidence of human occupation in prehistoric times can still be seen in the area. Signs of living and hunting for food, of the earliest settlement and farming are still evident here.

PREHISTORIC ROUTES AND TRADE

From the earliest times an east-west cross-country route through the glaciated valleys of the Aire and the Ribble carved a way across the Pennines. This route made use of the break in the hills, at a point called the Aire Gap, allowing a crossing of the hills to be made at a lower level than other crossings. This 'gap' is in effect a geological corridor through the Pennines near Skipton with the limestone uplands to the north and east and the predominantly millstone grit moors to the south and west. This prehistoric route followed the ridge of high ground that forms the watershed between the rivers Wharfe and Aire and

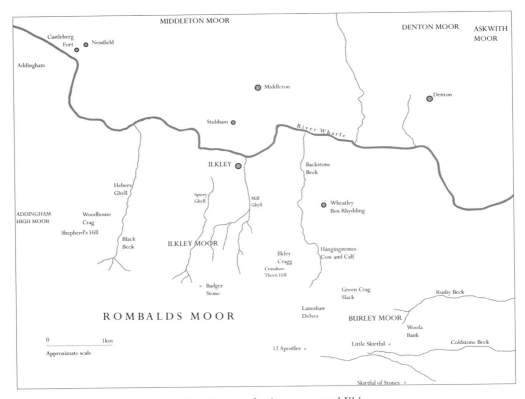

1   *Location map showing area around Ilkley.*

crossed Ilkley Moor and Rombald's Moor. This portion of the route, known locally as Rombald's Way, runs along the Chevin at Otley, across the length of Rombald's Moor and on westward past Ilkley to Addingham Moor and on through the Aire Gap. A local story that Rombald or Rumbold was a giant who lived on the moor (Bog 1904, 140) is an implausible explanation for the derivation of the name Rombald, which more likely derives from the de Romille family who, after the Conquest, held the Honour of Skipton. Their landholding extended from Skipton to the moorland near Silsden at the western edge of Rombald's Moor.

The earliest evidence of human occupation in the Ilkley area comes from a number of points along Rombald's Way where scatters of flint have been found, the earliest dating from 11,000 years ago. These finds show not only that has the area has been occupied since the earliest times but that trackways have been an important feature of the landscape since those days.

Much of the flint used to make tools and the debris of flint working which has been found was sourced from the Yorkshire Wolds, at the eastern end of the route, indicating the trade that was carried out along its entire length. Much later this prehistoric trackway may have been followed by the Romans, who built a road following a similar east-west cross-country route that linked forts along the way.

Crossing Rombald's Moor at Ilkley is another ancient route, running north-south, which fords the river Wharfe near the modern town and then branches north and north-east across the moorland which forms the watershed for the rivers Wharfe and Washburn and Nidd. Lithic scatters and tools have been found on this moorland to the north side of the river, on Middleton, Denton, Askwith and Snowden Moors. Similar scatters and tools dating from the Mesolithic and the Neolithic periods have been found at many different locations on the moorland on the south side of the valley at Rombald's, Ilkley and Burley Moors. There appears to have been a significant population here in Mesolithic times, with the original hunter-gatherer subsistence being gradually replaced by animal husbandry and a more settled agriculture over time. This change probably began around 5,000 B.C. but there is no clear-cut break between the Mesolithic and the Neolithic periods. The area of landscape relevant to prehistoric populations is quite extensive, but only a small portion of it, the area local to Ilkley, and some of the remains which survive there can be recounted here.

8,000 YEARS OF OCCUPATION

There is strong evidence for the production of stone tools in the locality. Finds indicate a more significant occupation here than would result from the occasional lost arrow head or discarded flint tool. A very significant Mesolithic flint-working site (since removed by gravel workings) was found on the bank of the Washburn River near Otley and evidence of flint working has also been found closer to Ilkley, immediately to the west of the present town on the ridge of Rombald's Moor, at Shepherd's Hill. More than 40 pieces of worked stone were recorded at a flint-working site here, and nearby, at High Crag, a collection of scrapers and a discarded flake knife have been found. Both these sites represent occupation in the late Mesolithic and Neolithic periods and provide evidence that imported flint was worked locally as the scrapers and other tools were made from flint brought from the Yorkshire Wolds, as well as chert found in the local glacial moraines (Cowling 1946, 20, 56). Some very good examples of Neolithic tools have also come from this area, including a horseshoe scraper, a small knife of pink flint, two well-made end scrapers and a barbed tanged point (Cowling 1946, 50). At Butts Hill at the eastern end of Rombald's Moor small lithic cores, scrapers and flake knives have been found over a large area (Cowling 1946, 53), again indicating a production site. A Neolithic polished stone axe made of local gritstone and a mace head were also found on Rombald's Moor (Cowling 1946, 35).

With a more settled agriculture in the Neolithic period came opportunities for technological experimentation and innovation, leading to an understanding of metallurgy and the production of bronze objects. Individual artefacts from various places on moorland above Ilkley show widespread Bronze-Age activity between 4,500 and 2,700 years ago. These include an axe from the south side of Rombald's Moor at East Morton

(Cowling 1946, 64), arrow points on Rombald's Moor (Cowling 1946, 67), fragments of beaker pottery on Baildon Moor, groove ware pottery on Ilkley Moor, and two late Bronze-Age swords found in gravel workings to the east of Ben Rhydding.

There are some areas of the moorland where terraces of flat ground cut into the valley sides. They are sheltered and have a plentiful water supply so were particularly favourable for occupation. One of these, Green Crag Slack, is at a height of about 310 metres above sea level, on Ilkley Moor at the eastern side of Ilkley. This area of terrace or plateau on the moor above Ilkley and Ben Rhydding is defined to the east and west by steep-sided narrow valleys in which streams called Coldstream and Backstone Becks flow. There may even have been a shallow lake here in Neolithic and early Bronze Age times (Boughey and Vickerman 2003, 9). It seems to have been occupied from the earliest times after the retreat of the glaciers until the Iron Age. Prehistoric remains here and at a similar site slightly further

2 *Looking west across moorland terrace at Green Crag Slack.*

east on Rombald's Moor at Woofa Bank are plentiful although, perhaps, have been studied relatively little. The remains are complex and indicate occupation over long periods of time but their interpretation is hindered by significant disturbance in more recent times.

Occupation at Green Crag Slack from the Mesolithic period is indicated by the discovery of a very good example of an 'angle graver' of black chert, a small chisel-type tool with a sharp tip that was used to engrave bone, stone or wood, along with various scrapers and hand axes (Cowling 1946, 21). Plentiful evidence of Neolithic lithic working has been found, with at least three sites at Green Crag Slack, and this includes evidence of the re-working of older flint tools. Finds from this location include a small three-sided drill with a worked finger grip possibly used to drill stones and bone for jewellery (Cowling 1946 52). Some fine tools have also been found at the western end of the ridge overlooking Green Crag Slack, Woofa Bank, including a long blade with teeth cut so that it might be used as a saw and tools which are thought to have been used for tattooing (Cowling 1946, 53).

The largest and most important early settlement locally is Green Crag Slack, which appears to be occupied through the Neolithic, Bronze-Age and Iron-Age periods. The main habitation was probably in the centre of the area, at the heart of a field system which once covered the whole terrace. In the 17th century stone was collected from the area, causing significant destruction to the remains, and today they are obscured by heather. But there are fragmentary remains of a field

system which seems to have extended over the whole area, with parts of field walls, an enclosure and hut sites. A cairnfield with stony banks and carved rocks extends between Green Crag Slack and Woofa Bank over an area which is more than two kilometres long and 360 metres wide. There are two adjoining walled field enclosures with further enclosures on the slope of Green Bank to the east and at the west of Green Crag Slack in the area above the Pancake Rock. Slightly further west at Stead Crag there are many short curved lengths of stony banks identified as field boundaries and these are closely associated with clearance cairns. The stony banks and walls, although they incorporate earth-fast stones, are mainly fragmentary tumbles of stone now. They would have been largely constructed with stone cleared from the areas to be enclosed with excess stone piled up to form clearance cairns.

The prehistoric settlement site at Woofa Bank was misinterpreted by antiquarians as a Roman encampment. There were once more extensive remains but in the 19th century they were significantly disrupted. Langdale described 'rude fire places constructed of stone, and filled with ashes' when the area of Woofa Bank was 'broken up' (1822, 325). However, some remains do survive at Woofa Bank where there is an incomplete oval-shaped, stony, rubble-walled enclosure measuring about eighty metres in length and fifty five metres wide. On the west side of this enclosure the remains are at their most substantial and the surviving wall incorporates a number of upright large boulders. The stonework appears to be coursed in places. There are carved rocks all with cup and ring marks within this enclosure, one incorporated into the wall. Within the enclosure, part of a curved ditch survives which is most likely a part of a hut circle and would originally have been about fifteen metres in diameter (NMR). The evidence from Green Crag Slack, Stead Crag and Woofa Bank is of a relatively settled population with extensive enclosure walls, hut circles and clearance cairns. These features show that the population had cleared areas of stone to create enclosures and fields for cultivation and animal husbandry some 4,500 to 2,700 years ago, during the Bronze Age.

In the moorland landscape above Ilkley, alongside their settlements and field systems, the prehistoric inhabitants left substantial remains of their burial practices in the period from the late Neolithic through the Bronze Age. On the east side of Rombald's Moor, on Ilkley and Burley Moor, there are several examples of cist burials, which are burial chambers made with flat stones, earthen barrows with upright 'kerb' stones, and stone circles. Prehistoric burial mounds were often located close to routeways and are certainly carefully positioned to be visible from a distance. There are the remains of large cairns on the highest point of Rombald's Moor, directly south of Ilkley, and at a high point to the south and west of Ilkley called Shepherds Hill. A large barrow stands on the rise of high ground above Ilkley Crags and to the south, and a smaller cairn on high ground to the south and east of Ilkley at Horncliff. Other cairns and barrows lie along the east-west routeway.

Notable examples of these burial monuments have been given the descriptive colloquial names of 'Skirtful of

3   Looking west across moorland terrace below High Crag.

Stones', the 'Little Skirtful', 'Grubstones' and the 'Twelve Apostles'. Two major cairns, known as the Great and Little Skirtful of Stones, are at the eastern side of Rombald's Moor and Burley Moor, together with three smaller burial cairns. The 'Great Skirtful' is a very large round burial cairn or barrow measuring about 26 metres in diameter and one and a half metres high; it is located on the main ridge of Rombald's Moor to the south of Green Crag Slack. The greater part of the

another round cairn, the 'Little Skirtful'. It is a similar height but, as its name suggests, is not as large. It is still of considerable size and may be more complete as it shows less sign of having been disturbed in the past. Cup marked stones have been found at the Little Skirtful of Stones (Boughey and Vickerman 2003, 16).

There are a number of other ring cairns in the area of the 'Great Skirtful' and the remains of other enclosures situated on the main ridge of Rombald's Moor. Further east, on Burley Moor close by a pathway, is the 'Grubstones', an embanked stone circle which is most likely a robbed-out cairn. The large cairn lies in the middle of an area where the natural formation of the moor makes a bottleneck about 400 yards wide. An excavation in 1846 revealed a cremation and what was called a flint 'spearhead' in the centre (Cowling 1946, 70), but part of the cairn was subsequently damaged by the construction of grouse butts. Stone circles excavated elsewhere have often produced evidence of cremations and in addition to their burial relevance may have served a variety of ceremonial functions, their significance possibly being redefined over time.

centre has been removed at some time in the past and a dump of material made on the south-west. A little to the north-west is

4   *Prehistoric ring cairn the 'Little Skirtful'.*

The Twelve Apostles Stone Circle is sited on a ridge to the side of Ilkley Crags close to a footpath crossing the moor from Ilkley to Bingley. There may originally have been more stones in the circle and three of them were still standing in 1914 (Cowling 1946, 70-1). The twelve surviving rough-worked stones measure over a metre high and form a circle about 15 metres across on a shallow bank, but the monument has been damaged through unauthorised attempts in the 1970s to stand the fallen stones upright. Winter and summer solstice celebrations have take place here in modern times and it is a site where sightings of strange lights and UFOs are said to abound.

CARVED ROCKS

One of the most interesting and important aspects of Rombald's Moor is the very many examples of rock carvings, also described as prehistoric rock art. Many hundreds of instances of 'cup and ring mark' carvings on rocks have been identified on loose boulders, earth-fast stones and on rock outcrops on the upland moors of Wharfedale, neighbouring Nidderdale and the Washborn Valley. There is a particular concentration of stones in the area lying on both sides of the river Wharfe at Rombald's Moor, Baildon Moor and Askwith Moor. Some carved stones are relatively easy to see, being close to modern footpaths, and others have been obscured by bracken or heather. A central carved depression or 'cup' may be surrounded by varying numbers of carved concentric circles, or 'rings'. Other stones have intricate patterns of 'ladders' and other curved or straight grooved lines. The repetition of some of the motifs of the carved patterns possibly indicates they are symbols of a language we no longer understand. What these patterns meant to the people who made them is something which has been subject to many interpretations. Some of the speculation has been very imaginative but theories centre on the concept that the markings are some sort of way marker, territorial boundary marker, signpost or stylised mapping information, and possibly represent maps of burials sites or other significant landscape features. Many of these stones are close to the route of Rombald's Way and they are in a landscape surrounded by barrow and cairn burial sites. Many theories about the carvings ascribe to them a magical or religious significance.

A few of these carved stones are incorporated into burial monuments or enclosure walling. In some instances they may just be stones re-used in these contexts; in other places they could be part of the original construction. The carved stones are thought to date from the Neolithic and Bronze-Age periods (about 6,000 to 2,700 years ago), although the chronology of the carved stones and the Neolithic and Bronze-Age settlement on the moor is difficult to disentangle. Currently it is thought that many of the earth-fast carved decorated stones on Rombald's Moor may date from the late Neolithic period and the early Bronze Age. Evidence from an excavation at Backstone on Ilkley Moor, where cup-marked rocks have been found in association with a stone-walled enclosure and fragments of grooved ware pottery, gave an early Bronze-Age date. Radiocarbon dating

5   *Cup and ring carved rock, the 'Badger Stone', on Ilkley Moor.*

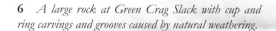

6   *A large rock at Green Crag Slack with cup and
ring carvings and grooves caused by natural weathering.*

of associated charcoal deposits was used (Vyner 2008, 5). The carved stone here is incorporated in walling, so dating it does not provide a definitive time for when the carving was made, but it is comparable with an emerging chronology for carved rocks in the North York Moors. A previously carved stone from the North York Moors is known to have been broken up and used to form the 'kerb' stones of a Bronze-Age burial cairn, and the newly exposed stone to have then been carved. This demonstrates that the rock carvings were a form of art or a language which was in use over a long period, and that over time the 'message' of one carving became irrelevant or was certainly superseded.

The cup and ring can be seen as a decorative motif so the carvings may have had artistic cultural meaning from earliest times, or the motifs may have had a more practical purpose related to the mapping or passing on of important information to those who made the carvings. Over time the motifs may have lost their ability to convey their original practical or spiritual information but retained their resonance as a decorative motif and some of the popular names given to these ancient stones overlay more recent cultural and religious references. The most famous of the Ilkley carved stones is the 'Swastika Stone' on the edge of Woodhouse Crag. This carving, which is thought by some to be later than many of the other carvings on the moor (possibly dating from the Iron Age), has ten cup marks inside a continuous curved groove and there are eight other cup marks and two basins. The cup marks form two lines crossing at right angles

7   Carved rock the 'swastika stone' at Woodhouse Crag overlooking Ilkley. The Victorian copy of the design can be seen on the smaller stone.

8 *Detail of the carving on the 'swastika' stone.*

9 *Victorian copy of carving on the 'swastika' stone.*

and the encompassing curved line around them forms curved 'arms'. A copy of the 'swastika' motif was made on the adjacent rock in Victorian times. Very similar carving appears on several rocks at Val Camonica, Italy, where the carving has become known as the 'camunian rose' and been used as the symbol of Lombardy. Other very similar carvings have been found in Sweden.

Some of the carved rocks have been re-used and are found in stone walls. A cup-marked stone has been re-used as one of a pair of gateposts, both of which are now lying unused on the ground to the west of the 'Swastika Stone'.

To the east of the 'Swastika Stone' there used to be a concentration of carved rocks together with some upright stones, possibly forming a cairn and an enclosure extending along the plateau. These included stones described by Romilly Allen as 'some of the finest sculptured stones near Ilkley' (1879, 20). In the 1890s the Panorama Reservoir and the houses at the end of Panorama Drive were built and many of these stones were lost. The Panorama stone, which is covered in the most intricate cup and ring mark carvings was saved from this fate. This particular stone has a

10   *Cup-marked rock, once re-used as a gate-post and now recumbent.*

11   *Some carvings on the Panorama stone.*

somewhat chequered history having been purchased in 1890 by Dr Fletcher Little, then physician at Ben Rhydding Hydro, from the purchaser of the building plot. The stone was move from the moor and broke into pieces at some time in the past. In 1892 the Ilkley Local Board agreed to locate it at a site opposite St Margaret's Church in Queen's Road where, in truth, this important stone has been sadly neglected. The fact that some of the carvings on the Panorama stone are not as intricate as the majority of the work and could be later imitations was noted in 1946 (Cowling 1946, 88), and more recently it has been suggested that the ladder motif on the stone may have been added in Victorian times (Gavin Edwards, *Ilkley Gazette* 2006). He compared drawings made of the stone which may indicate the ladder was a latter addition, and noted a comment made by the bailiff of Ilkley Moor, Mr Gill, that a workman employed at the Semon Convalescent Home from 1872-3, Ambrose Collins, would 'spend most of his leisure time carving and ornamenting the rocks near the home, evidently hoping that at some future time they would be discovered and become famous'. There are examples of later carvings being added to stones, and of modern graffiti, but whether this particular carving was done by Collins is conjecture.

12   *Carved rock the 'Idol Stone' and associated stones, at Green Crag Slack.*

13   *The 'Haystack Rock'.*

At Green Crag Slack a stone known as the Idol Stone sits within a small cluster of rocks, some of which are also carved and may be the scattered remains of a cairn. The carvings on this stone are unusually regular and are deep, closely spaced, cup marks in four regular lines. One of the lines of cups is surrounded by a groove and there is a curved groove along the edge of the stone.

The Haystack Rock is a very prominent large rock on Pancake Ridge, to the west of Green Crag Slack. The rock is covered with carvings, about seventy cups, some with rings, and many carved linear grooves, although some of the grooves are the result of weathering.

A carved rock called the Planets Rock, on the edge of the plateau of Green Crag Slack, has 13 cups, nine of which have rings, together with grooves, including a grove which run around the edge of the stone.

Another carved stone on the edge of a terrace at Pipers Crag overlooks the river Wharfe west of Ilkley, where the river turns quite abruptly towards the north after running west-east. This stone has 32 cup marks, some with rings and grooves.

There are many instances of carved rocks and a very few are illustrated here. Study of the stones and the prehistoric landscape is ongoing and, although a gazetteer of the stones has been compiled, new examples of carved rocks continue to be recorded. There is still much to be studied and understood regarding the earliest inhabitants of the moorland above Ilkley and the enigmatic carvings they left behind.

14 *Detail of cup and ring carvings on the 'Haystack Rock'.*

15 *Carvings on the 'Planets Rock' at Green Crag Slack.*

16 *Carved cup and ring marks on a rock at Pipers Crag.*

17   *Looking across the moorland terrace at Woofa Bank.*

THE BRIGANTES: IRON-AGE ROMANO-BRITISH LIFE

Before the Romans much of the Pennine uplands in Yorkshire were occupied by groups of people collectively known as the Brigantes. Their territory covered a large part of northern England and the extensive area to each side of the Pennines, with the exception of a large area, now in East Yorkshire, which belonged to the Parisii. The history of the Brigantes is not known in great detail but they are thought to have been a confederation of many smaller Iron-Age groups.

Rural life before and after the arrival of the Romans may, in many respects, not have been significantly different for the Brigantes. Farmsteads were often sited within enclosures sometime defined by an encircling ditch, inside which would be a

number of circular huts. Settlements like this were occupied in the Iron Age and on into the Romano-British period. The huts were built with wooden posts and mud and daub walls or else stones may have been used to form the base of the walls. The stone, cleared from fields, was also used to establish boundaries between fields. Some of the enclosures would have been used to keep cattle.

Grain grown on these farmsteads was hand-milled using quern stones to make a coarse flour. In Yorkshire, beehive querns, small hand-operated corn mills, are a characteristic indicator of Iron-Age settlement and they are particularly prevalent in the valleys of the rivers Wharfe and Aire where they were made from local millstone grit. Although their typology has yet to be fully refined, they seem to have been used from about 400 B.C. and remained in use until Roman rotary querns were introduced in the 1st century A.D. Some of the areas of prehistoric settlement on the moorland above Ilkley are thought to have been occupied in the Iron Age. Beehive querns have been recovered from the area and some are known to have come from Green Crag Slack (Cowling 1946, 159).

West of Ilkley, at nearby Castleberg, on a high spur at Nessfield is the site of a defended Iron-Age settlement with a field system close by. It is a naturally defended promontory to the east and traces of a rampart and deep ditch survive of the southern defence. The site, like Green Crag Slack, may also have known earlier occupation since a Bronze-Age urn and flints have been found in the vicinity. It was mistaken for a Roman camp by antiquarian historians Langdale (1822, 325) and Whitaker (1878, 287). There are other sites with the fragmented remains of Iron-Age farming on nearby moorland at Addingham Low Moor and Denton Moor. A hoard of Iron-Age coins dating from A.D. 10-40 has been found relatively recently near to Silsden on the south side of Rombald's Moor.

In the 2nd century A.D. Roman writer Ptolemy listed nine towns in the north of England belonging to the Brigantes, and the list included *Olicana*, which has been identified with Ilkley (*see* p.27). Antiquarians and historians have tended to accept this identification until relatively recent times but it is now thought *Olicana* is mistakenly identified as Ilkley and was instead Elslack. Importantly, though, even if Ilkley were not *Olicana*, and so not listed, it is known Ptolemy's list was not exhaustive, so Ilkley may still have been the site of a Brigantian settlement.

Historians have hinted at the possibility there could have been an Iron-Age settlement in the area occupied by the modern town of Ilkley prior to the Roman's use of the site as a fort. They suggest the vallum and ditch of the fort had previously formed defences of 'the ancient Brigantian town' (Cowling 1946, 160, citing John Holmes in a letter to the *Ilkley Observer*).

However, excavations at the site of the fort did not reveal anything indicating occupation before the Roman fort, although this is not conclusive.

Following the first arrival of the Romans in England, the Briganti were not mentioned among the named rulers who surrendered to Claudius at Colchester in A.D. 43, but in the A.D. 50s Queen Cartimandua is known to have been their ruler. She and her husband Venutius were described by Tacitus as loyal to the Romans, and initially the Briganti were regarded as 'client rulers' by the Romans, maintaining some sort of alliance with the Romans rather than opposition to them. Disputes amongst the Brigantes later led to an uprising in A.D. 69, when Venutius, no longer married to Queen Cartimandua, led a rebellion against her and against Roman rule. The Romans turned their attentions to subduing this opposition but it appears that it took some time to subjugate the Brigantes since it was A.D. 79 before the Roman governor of Britain, Agricola, was able to return to the conquest of the North which he had completed, at least for the time being, by the end of his governorship in A.D. 84.

Two

ROMAN FORT AT ILKLEY

The Roman strategy for imposing their rule over an area was to establish a network of routes crossing the country at strategic points, with auxiliary forts lining these routes. Supplies and communications could thus be maintained over a large area. The fort established at Ilkley was one of these, built at a strategically important position in the mid-Pennines at the junction of the Roman roads from Ribchester to York and Manchester to Aldborough, with another road linking Ilkley with Bainbridge. The Romans built a string of forts and a road which followed a similar east-west line to Rombald's way. On the east side of the Pennines they established major forts at Brough on Humber, Malton and York, with smaller forts at Ilkley and Elslack linking to a more important fort at Ribchester on the west side of the Pennine ridge. The first fort at Castleford, located to control an important crossing point on the river Aire, on the route between the Roman towns of York and Lincoln, was also established at this time. These forts, in Brigantian territory, would have acted as bases from which rebellion could be subdued. Tacitus,

a Roman writer and son-in-law of Agricola, the Roman general and governor of Britain, has provided a record of the Roman campaign in Britain. It has been surmised that the Romans, as they extended their control northwards in the last quarter of the 1st century, would probably have proceeded northward on two fronts, one on each side of the Pennines. The establishment of smaller outposts along a cross-Pennine route was critical to allow for communication between the two wings of the army. The fort at Ilkley may have been established with this precise military purpose, and forts at regular intervals along the Roman road system allowed a lookout to be kept for potential trouble in newly conquered territory.

Ilkley presented an eminently suitable site for a fort, lying in a sheltered valley at a fordable point across the river Wharfe. The crucial factor was Ilkley's position at the junction of two important Roman routes, one east-west across the Pennines and the other north-south. The east-west routeway, used in prehistory and followed in more recent times by the Leeds-Liverpool Canal and the A59 road, is a very important connecting route between the east and the west sides of the country. The fort was built in a position to command the ford over the river Wharfe, on a plateau between two narrow valleys with streams flowing into the river. It was maintained almost continuously throughout the Roman period, indicating the importance of this east-west supply route through the Aire Gap, which linked a line of forts from Ribchester to Brough on Humber.

ROMAN ROADS

The north-south route from Manchester to Ilkley, and north-eastwards to Aldborough near Boroughbridge, or north to Bainbridge, is thought to have crossed the Wharfe by a 'deep stony ford' at a point not far from the old bridge (Wardell 1881, 14). It is clear that these roads were well built and continued in use long after the Romans had left. John Warburton's map of Yorkshire, surveyed in 1720, provides good detail of the roads, and notes that 'this Roman way extends from Manchester in Lancashire unto Aldborough near Borrow bridge, is all paved with stone and near eight yards wide'. The road out of Ilkley to Manchester is described as traversing Rombald's Moor and 'the slope of the Weary Hill on the lines of the road from Keighley behind Wells House at Ilkley, but in a more direct line' (Norton Dickons 1898, 250). Portions of the road leading northwards from the ford at Ilkley are reported to have been seen at the site of a brickworks on the north bank of the river Wharfe and further north at Middleton Lodge (Collyer 1885, 29).

18 *The modern path down from Weary Hill towards Ilkley.*

The Roman east-west route linked a line of forts from Ribchester and Elslack to Ilkley and then crossed the Chevin and Bramhope Moor to the fort at Adel, joining York Gate on the Roman route in the east to York. Warburton's map notes where this road enters Yorkshire from the west: 'This Roman Way goes to York, and for the most part is visible, being paved with stone throughout.' In 1736 part of the route was described as coming from the west to Gisburn, then across Rombald's Moor to the fort at Ilkley (Drake 1736). Portions of the route from Littleborough (near Rochdale) to Ilkley were still passable by foot until the mid-18th century, although it was then in a ruinous condition in places. Elsewhere it was incorporated with the highway or

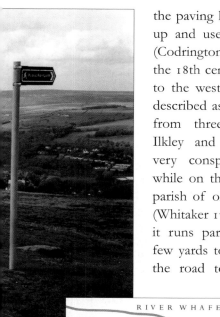

the paving had been taken up and used for building (Codrington 1919). Later in the 18th century, the route to the west of Ilkley was described as 'still traceable from three miles from Ilkley and then appears very conspicuous for a while on the moor in the parish of old Addingham' (Whitaker 1773, 193). Here it runs parallel to and a few yards to the south of the road to Skipton (by Cross Bank and over Draughton Heights), passing some distance south of the town and eventually on to Ribchester. It was reported that a raised paved Roman road, though overgrown, could be seen on Rombald's Moor, the route 'keeping on the shelve of the hills, to avoid the cliffs and the morasses to either side of it, pointing directly to the valley of the Wharfe and the village of Ilkley within it' (Whitaker 1773, 192), but it was destroyed in the 19th century (Norton Dickon 1898, 220), and no known remains of this road survive above ground on Ilkley or Rombald's Moor. Elsewhere, portions of Roman road can be seen as earthworks and these have been excavated along the route. On the east side of Ilkley a section of the road with a bank and ditch survived as an earthwork until it was destroyed by a modern housing development. It was seen when a service trench was excavated in the housing estate. Part of the route

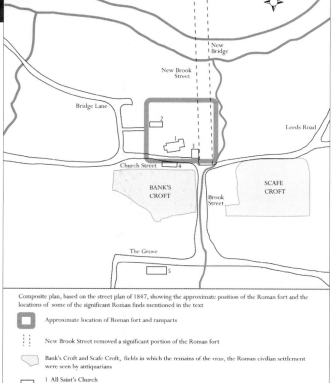

Composite plan, based on the street plan of 1847, showing the approximate position of the Roman fort and the locations of some of the significant Roman finds mentioned in the text

Approximate location of Roman fort and ramparts

New Brook Street removed a significant portion of the Roman fort

Bank's Croft and Scafe Croft, fields in which the remains of the *vicus*, the Roman civilian settlement were seen by antiquarians

1 All Saint's Church
2 Manor House Museum
3 Wheatsheaf Public House (now demolished)
4 Rose and Crown Coaching Inn, Church Street
5 Congregational Church, The Grove

19 *Composite plan showing the approximate position of the Roman fort and the location of some of the significant Roman finds mentioned in the text including the fields to the south of the fort in which remains of the vicus were seen by antiquarians.*

was examined before a modern by-pass at Addingham was constructed and the road was found to have been heavily robbed of stone (YAS 1987-8). In Ilkley there are no visible traces of the Roman road itself, but the remains of a cobbled road 12 feet wide were seen when drainage works were done in the yard of the *Rose and Crown* on Church Street (Norton Dickon 1898, 253).

The reason for a fort being established at Ilkley in the 1st century A.D. may have been the communications route between the Roman centres either side of the Pennines. Ilkley was unusual, however, in that it was altered and re-built but appears to have continued in use for almost the whole of the Roman period. Elsewhere, as strategic changes were made, forts were left without a role to play and were abandoned, the one at Castleford, for example, being abandoned at the beginning of the 2nd century. Elslack may have been abandoned in the middle of the 2nd century. Ilkley may have been maintained because it was at the crossing of two major routes and so enjoyed greater strategic significance.

DEVELOPMENT OF THE ROMAN FORT

Several stages of development are known to have taken place for the military fort. The first fort was built in A.D. 79-80 while Agricola was Roman governor. It was constructed mainly from wood, with defences formed by a wide ditch approximately six metres deep and an earth rampart, founded on stone, built with the earth dug out of from the ditch and then piled up on the inside to form a high rampart five to six metres wide

(Hartley 1966, 41). On top of this was a palisade and walkway along which sentries would have patrolled.

Within the area defended by the fort, buildings were constructed of timber. These included a headquarters with a courtyard surrounded by office buildings and the commandant's house, along with the hospital and granaries for storing food such as wheat, barley, peas and beans. These were located centrally, with the barracks, workshops and stables occupying the edges of the fort. The buildings are not thought to have been greatly altered, apart from the *praetorium*, or commander's house. The fort was occupied for most of the Roman period although it may have been evacuated and temporarily abandoned in the early 2nd century, as were a number of forts, when Hadrian took the decision to build a frontier further north.

It is reasonably certain that the first fort was not destroyed by enemy action but was deliberately levelled, including the ramparts, and it was not long before a new fort with earthen rampart was built, possibly as a response to a Brigantian rebellion thought to have occurred in A.D. 154-5. We know the new fort was occupied at a date sometime between A.D. 161 and 169 (Hartley 1966, 32) because an inscribed Roman stone was found re-used in the tower of the church. The inscription was dedicated at Ilkley by Caecilius, *praefectus* (commander) of a cohort and honours Marcus Aurelius and Lucius Verus, who succeeded as co-Emperors in 161 before Lucius Verus died in A.D. 169. The fort at Ilkley must have been re-built and occupied in this period if a stone was inscribed to these leaders.

PRO SALVTE IMPERATORVM
CAES AVGG ANTONINI ET
VERI IOVI DILECT CAECILIVS
LVCANVS PRAEF COH translates
as 'For the health of the emperors, the
August Caesars Antoninus and Verus,
beloved of Jupiter, Caecilius Lucanus,
prefect of the cohort [made this].

The new fort was also made of wood
and is known to have been used for
around thirty years. The garrison was
almost certainly a *cohort equitata*, composed
of part infantry, part cavalry, perhaps
the Lingones (Hartley 1966, 42). It was
destroyed by fire and it has been suggested
this occurred during the documented
Brigantian rebellion in A.D. 196-7 (MM).
The fort at Ilkley was re-garrisoned almost
immediately. The Roman Emperor Severus
set about re-establishing control of
Britain, appointing a new governor Virius
Lupus, and Ilkley was one of the first forts
to be re-built, in 197-8. A Roman stone,
reportedly dug up in the church, testifies
to the foundation of this replacement
fort. The stone (now lost) was noted by
the historian Camden in or near the south-
east buttress of the church, and dates to
*c.*179. The inscription read:

IM. SEVERVS. AVG ET
ANTONINVS CAES. DESTINATVS
RESTITVERVNT. CV_RANTE VIRIO
LVPO LEG. EORVM PR. PR. Langdale
1822, 324, translates as 'For the emperors
Severus Augustus and Antoninus Caesar,
fixed and restored under the care of
Virius Lupus, their pro-praetorian legate'.
The stone was taken to Middleton Lodge
and by 1881 the inscription was described
as 'lost or illegible' (Wardell 1881, 17).

It was common for forts to be rebuilt
and the replacement was constructed in
stone, the defences strengthened when
parts of the earlier rampart were cut away
to insert a stone defensive wall and stone
walls being built around the rampart.
Stone was used for the first time in the
construction of buildings inside the fort,
and stone sill walls (foundations) have been
found. This third fort is thought to have
been occupied continuously through the
3rd century. It was almost certainly used to
garrison a *cohors equitata*, though probably
not the Lingones (Hartley 1966, 42). It
has been suggested the western rampart
may have been largely reduced during this
period, but no evidence has been found for
destruction which might have terminated
occupation here, and it seems likely that
the reduction of the rampart took place
during the next phase of occupation, when
more general levelling is known to have
taken place.

The last phase of the fort is likely
to have been associated with a more
general re-organisation by the Romans
under Constantius in the 4th century.
There is evidence for the continued use
of the stables so it is likely that the unit
garrisoned here was at least in part a
cavalry one. The appearance of the fort
seems to have changed markedly in this
period, presumably as the need for strong
defences diminished. The rampart was
levelled and the fort wall was almost
certainly free-standing with simplified
gates (Hartley 1966, 42). These alterations
allowed for additional space inside the fort
which made it possible for buildings to
be extended towards the defences. There
was room for a new larger *praetorium* and

at least one building in the *praetentura* (the front part of camp). The buildings were still constructed on a regular alignment and decorated by external colonnades. Later in the century an extra granary was added to the central range of buildings and the stabling was demolished (Hartley 1966, 43). By this time the type of unit garrisoned is unlikely to have included cavalry horses.

The fort continued in full occupation into the late 4th century or early 5th century. Buildings inside the walls were still being renewed and repaired in the late 4th century, including the suite of rooms in the commandant's house, which had under-floor heating. A building was constructed on the site of the stables although it was not on the same regular alignment. A precise end-date for the Roman occupation of the fort is not known but it seems Ilkley was the only fort in West Yorkshire to have been used throughout most of the Roman period. Elsewhere fort defences were filled in and buildings demolished as the military situation changed.

The site was one which had natural defensive qualities. It had the river Wharfe to the north, with tributary streams to the east and west. These are no longer obvious, the water being diverted and channelled mainly out of sight. In the middle of the 18th century the historian Whitaker noted that 'The ground is admirably defended to the north by the Wharfe and by two brooks to the sides. The western brook has had half its waters diverted into another channel, but must have been a lively current before this and given additional natural strength to the

brow … and the eastern channel is still extremely brisk.' (Whitaker 1773, 195) When Whitaker visited Ilkley he could see the whole of the fort in outline and he noted the north–west corner of the wall of the station 'is easily discovered under the turf along the whole verge of the brow being of the rough flagstones of the country' (1773, 195). In the early 19th century another historian, Langdale, described the outline of the fort on three sides as 'very entire' and sited on 'a steep and lofty bank, having the river Wharfe on the north, and the deep channel of a brook immediately on the east and west; the southern boundary seems to have coincided with the present street'. He could see very clearly 'the foundations of the fortress bedded in indissoluble mortar' and the 'remains of Roman brick, glass, and earthenware, every where, appear on the edges or the brow' (Langdale 1822, 324-5).

Much of the platform on which the fort had been constructed probably survived until a new bridge was constructed over the Wharfe in 1904 and New Brook Street was developed. The new road, measuring 50 feet wide, was built through the fort, removing a good portion of the eastern rampart (Woodward 1926, 152). Today there are still some visible remains of the fort but much of the area previously occupied by it has been landscaped and All Saints parish church sits within. The earthwork remains of the northern edge can still be seen although lowered from the defensive height the rampart once reached. Only a short stretch of wall close to the north-western corner of the rampart is still visible. A series of

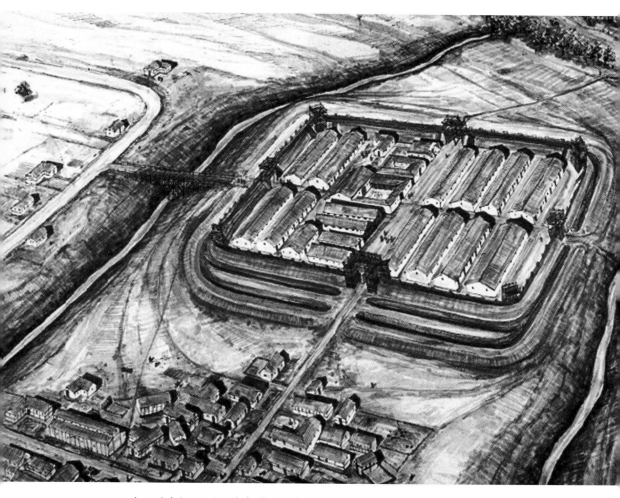

20 *An artist's impression of the Roman fort and vicus, or civilian settlement nearby, to the south.*

interpretation panels prepared by the West Yorkshire Archaeological Service is on the site.

It is apparent from the writings of antiquarians that Roman finds were abundant at Ilkley, but that many artefacts found at the fort and elsewhere in Ilkley in the past were not collected, or were subsequently lost. Quantities of coins, querns, bricks, glass and earthenware were seen behind the church, 'but are now lost' (Wardell 1881, 15). 'Bits of red samian ware,

fragments of glass, tiles, pottery and bones were seen protruding from the ramparts or having fallen into the brook below' (Speight 1900, 188). It was not until the 20th century that there was systematic examination of any part of the fort. An excavation took place over a number of seasons in the years 1919-21, and in 1962 a more comprehensive investigation was carried out. An excavation within the church tower in 1983 found deposits associated with the fort about 1.5 metres below the nave floor.

ROMAN SOLDIERS
AT ILKLEY

The fort at Ilkley, in common with known others in West Yorkshire, at Castleford, Adel, Slack, Wetherby, Roall, Burghwallis and Newton Kyme, seems to have been manned by auxiliaries. These were recruits from various parts of the Roman empire who would complete their military service as a means by which to become citizens. The name of one garrison at Ilkley is known for certain as there is an inscribed stone and undated stamped tiles bearing the name of the 2nd cohort of Lingones, who must have occupied the fort at some time in the 2nd century. These men were recruited from Langrer in eastern France and local Britons may also have been added to the strength. They were a cohors equitata, a mixed unit of infantry and cavalry, with a nominal strength of 360 infantry and 120 cavalry. It is not know exactly when or for how long they were based at Ilkley. Units with cavalry needed extra space to stable the horses. In Britain they usually occupied forts measuring between 3.25 and 3.75 acres (Hartley 1966, 27). Antiquarians estimated the size of the fort from their observations of surviving earthworks to be 160 by 100 yards, or 3.3 acres (Wardell 1881, 15). The fort was estimated by the first excavators as smaller than this, at around 2.23 acres (Woodward 1925, 157), but the more recent excavation in 1960 arrived at an estimate of around 3.23 acres (Hartley 1966, 29). This identifies Ilkley as a similarly sized fort to the one at Slack which also garrisoned a cohors equitata.

That a cohort of the Lingones was quartered in Ilkley is indicated by an inscription found on an altar stone, inscribed by the Captain of the cohort of the Lingones to Verbeia, possibly the goddess of the river Wharfe: 'VERBIAE SACRUM CLODIUS FRONTO D PRAEF. COH II LINGON', that is 'To sacred Verbia. Clodus Fronto, Prefect of Cohort, Second Legion', although Camden thought the inscription read 'VERBEIAE SACRUM CLODIVS FRONTO PRAEF COH II LINGONES'. Thoresby transcribed the final words as 'P LINGONES', whereas Warburton, who made the first drawing of the stone in 1718, read them as 'P LINDON' and thought it was the first and not the second cohort of Lingones whose commander had dedicated the altar to Verbeia (Speight 1900, 189). The earliest report of the inscribed altar is from the 16th century, when the poet Edward Fairfax saw the altar stone 'standing in water in a house' (Collyer 1885, 26), and in 1830 it was described as having been taken out of the river Wharfe (Shaw 1830, 73), although Camden reported he had seen it holding up the stairs of a house. It was taken to Middleton Lodge in 1608 (Collyer 1885, 26) and by 1822 the inscription had become illegible due to weathering (Langdale 1822, 324).

Another inscription suggests that another cohort may have been garrisoned at Ilkley. An inscribed tombstone of a soldier was found in a garden wall at Ilkley in the 19th century by the Reverend Mr Carr and then taken to the vicarage at Arncliffe. This inscription read, 'DM PVDE JESSEI LEG II A' (Whitaker 1878, 287), which translates as 'To the spirits of the departed and to Pudens, *tesserarius* (and) soldier of the Second Augustan

Legion'. The stone commemorated the death of Pudens Jesseus and is thought to date from Severus's reign (late 1st century to early 2nd century). This soldier held the rank of *tesserarius*, a cohort officer, and belonged to the 2nd Augustan legion. This may indicate the presence of this legion at Ilkley, although it is not thought to have served in the north of England until later in the Roman period.

THE NAME OF THE ROMAN TOWN

In the 2nd century A.D. the Roman writer Ptolemy listed nine towns in the north of England belonging to the Brigantes, although it is now known they were in control of more towns than are represented on the list (which included Aldborough, Adel, Castleshaw (Greater Manchester), Catterick, Lancaster, and York). One of them was called Olicana and the antiquary William Camden was the first to interpret this location as Ilkley. Historians have tended to accept this identification until relatively recent times. The association is of such long standing and is used today in the names of local shops and businesses so it is likely to persist whether or not it is historically accurate. Many attempts have been made to derive the modern place-name from this Latin name and link it back to a pre-existing British name. For example, Speight suggests it may come from Ol meaning station and y ceann, meaning rocky promontory or headland, possibly referring to the Cow and Calf Rocks (1900, 186). Collyer suggests a similar derivation, given that Llecan was an Old British word for rock (1885, 1).

21 *Carved Roman altar stone (later re-used as a church window arch).*

Modern scholarship has cast significant doubt on the identification of *Olicana* with Ilkley and it is suggested *Olicana* should be regarded as the name of the Roman fort at Elslack, south of Skipton, since *Olicana* may have been a misnaming of *Olenacum*, now ascribed to Elslack (NMR). An alternative Roman name for Ilkley of *Verbeia* has been proposed by Rivet and Smith, who suggest that an altar found at Ilkley may provide the significant clue to the original name (Rivet and Smith 1979, 43). The altar (*see* p.26) was dedicated to *Verbeia*, goddess of the river Wharfe, and as many Roman place-names are derived from the local deity it is possible *Verbeia* may have provided the Roman name for Ilkley.

Another sculpted stone, also part of a carved Roman altar, was found incorporated in the fabric of the church tower and it has been thought to represent *Verbeia* the goddess. Wardell describes seeing a carved stone in the north wall of the interior of the church tower and interprets the figure as Hercules strangling serpents (Wardell 1881, 16 and Whitaker 1878, 283). By 1900 a plaster cast had been made of the stone and it was on display in the church. Speight describes it as portraying a human figure holding two serpent-like objects, but notes that Gough and Camden have taken the figure to represent *Verbeia*. There is no inscription, but the 'serpents' may represent the flow of the river and the figure may symbolise the Wharfe (Speight 1900, 190). It has also been suggested that carving represented an earth goddess, Demeter, or her daughter, Persephone, holding a torch in either hand. Whether or not this carved stone was intended to represent the goddess, it does not weaken the argument

for *Verbeia* as the Roman name of Ilkley, the more compelling evidence coming from the inscribed altar stone.

ROMAN CIVILIAN SETTLEMENT OR VICUS

The lengthy occupation of the fort over a period of four centuries means it can be said with certainty that a civilian settlement or *vicus* would have developed nearby. A feature of Roman forts was the development of a civilian settlement to provide services and trade with the fort. It was a place where soldiers' families lived and would grow over time into a market town. However, since no systematic excavation has taken place, little can be said of the extent and character of this civilian settlement with certainty. It is generally agreed the *vicus* would have been located to the south of and close to the fort, but the exact location and layout remains

22 *Family group carved on a memorial stone.*

uncertain. The settlement is thought to have been located along the main east-west road in the area of what is now The Grove. Woodward, who carried out the excavation of the fort at the beginning of the 20th century, used a map of Roman finds from Ilkley compiled by Isaac Dean, along with published sources, and noticed all the finds could be plotted within close range to the south of the fort. Additional significant finds are located further away from the fort at the bottom of Cowpasture Road, in Tivoli Place, on Wells Road, Chapel Lane and at the site of the former gasworks to the east.

In the 18th century the historian Whitaker stated that the Roman town was built very near the fort along the course of the road from the west, in 'Bank's croft, Scafe croft and some adjoining closes', where 'fragments of brick, remarkably red have been frequently dug up and the foundations of the houses remain very visible at present' (Whitaker 1773, 196). These 'crofts' or fields lay to the east and west of Brook Street, in the area to the south of Church Street, south of the fort. It is not certain the foundations visible at the time were of Roman date, but it is likely as Roman finds have been made within this area from the 16th century onwards. A very considerable number of Roman artefacts of domestic character were discovered here during the period in the 19th century when the town was developed and the railway constructed, confirming the existence of the *vicus* in the area to the south of the fort.

With no systematic excavation, the character of the settlement can only be indicated by some of these finds. Memorial stones recovered during building work in

23 *Memorial tombstone for a Cornovian woman.*

the 19th century provide clear evidence of Roman civilian life in Ilkley. One shows a family group and the other a Cornovian woman who may have been the wife of a soldier (Manor Museum, Ilkley). (The Cornovii were another British tribe from Shropshire.) This stone was found in the yard of the *Rose and Crown*, Church Street in 1884.

The stone carved with the family group was found in 1867 while excavating the foundations of the Congregational Church in The Grove. It measured 5 feet 8 inches by

3 feet 4 inches and was sadly broken in two by workmen, although it was later pieced together. These memorial stones are now on display in the Manor House Museum. The large tombstones may or may not have been found in their original locations but an apparently undisturbed cremation burial was uncovered at the junction of Springs Lane and Cowpasture Road and another in Tivoli Place. Another burial was found in 1887 in a field thought to be near Bridge Lane. More recently, in 1998 a burial was found during an excavation on land to the rear of Glovers Garage on Bridge Lane, where two ditches at the western extent of the fort were also found.

Other sculpted stones, as well as many examples of pottery, glass, coins and Roman quern stones, have been found in the town but many objects have been dispersed. The fate of some items seems very sad, a fine, whole vase found during the building of the railway station, for example, being broken by workmen (Whitaker 1878, 283). Writing in 1881 the historian Wardell notes that the 'foundations of some building of the Roman period were discovered in excavating for a house on the north-east side of the village. These stones were immense in size, laid in circular form; half of the circle was uncovered and the stones broken up for use in road making.' (1881, 15) There may have been a pottery kiln nearby since quantities of pottery waste were found in 1886 in the area behind the station. The construction of a railway line from Ilkley to Skipton took a line straight through the middle of the area where the *vicus* is thought to have been sited, and would certainly have taken away significant remains of the Roman settlement. Now the railway line itself has been removed.

Three

MEDIEVAL ILKLEY

AN EARLY CHURCH AND DECORATED CROSSES

Many of the villages in Wharfedale close to Ilkley are mentioned in the Domesday survey and may date from Saxon times. Examples are Beamsley, Addingham, Nessfield, Stubham, Middleton, Denton, Askwith, Clifton, Farnley and Leathley (on the north side of the river) and (on the south side) Burley, Menston, Otley and Hawksworth, along with Ilkley itself. The name 'Ilkley' derives from the Old English and translates as *Yllica's* or *Illica's 'ley'* (meaning wood or clearing). Many of the village settlements with the oldest origins are those located on higher ground, the area occupied in prehistoric times, rather than in the valley. Lying at a crossing of two important cross-country routes, Ilkley would have retained some importance even after the Romans had left. Little is known of the elements which formed Ilkley at this time, no clear evidence of a Saxon manor house having been found, nor of any farmsteads or cottages built in the period. Something can be inferred about Ilkley from the records of the Archbishop of York's Wharfedale estates, the later record of the Domesday Survey, and from the very fine surviving sculpted crosses which are thought to date from the ninth century.

At the time of the Domesday survey of 1085, two separate land holdings included land at Ilkley. The spelling of Ilkley in Domesday and other historic documents is varied and it appears as Ilkley, Ilecliue, Illecluie, Illielei and Illieleia. Firstly, Ilkley is mentioned amongst the extensive holdings of William de Percy along with the fact that before the Conquest the manor, including a church with a resident priest, was held by a Saxon thane called Gamel. Additionally, part of Ilkley is referred to in Domesday amongst the holdings of the manor of Otley, which was held in 1085 by the Archbishop of York. An ecclesiastical estate in Wharfedale may have been held by the archbishop from as early the seventh century. A Bishop's Palace was established at Otley and a Saxon church built there. A specific documentary reference to Ilkley as part of this ecclesiastical estate dates from the early 11th century, when the Archbishop of York's ownership of the

24 *Three carved stone cross shafts standing in the churchyard in the 19th century.*

crosses show that in the eighth to ninth century there is very likely to have been a Christian burial ground and a church at Ilkley, although they could have been used as preaching crosses which served as the focus of Christian worship before a church was built.

William Camden saw the three large crosses at the end of the 16th century, described them as lying in the church yard, and mistakenly thought they were Roman (Le Patourel 1968, 15). A small fragment of another cross was found in the foundations of a cottage opposite the church in 1868 and shows a human figure and ornamental scroll work (Whitaker 1878, 285). The three crosses formerly stood in different parts of the church yard and at some point one of them appears to have been used as a gatepost at the south gateway (Le Patourel 1968, 15). Speight writes that both of the shorter crosses 'have long time served ignominiously as gate posts to the church yard' (Speight 1900, 198). The crosses were placed upright, together in the south side of the churchyard, by the vicar John Snowden in the mid-19th century (Shuttleworth 1882) and a photograph of them became a popular Ilkley postcard. Speight writing in 1900 suggested the crosses should be found a place inside the church or a special annex be built to house them, as was done for the carved crosses at the church at Ruthwell in Scotland (1900, 198), but it was sometime before they were housed indoors in the church tower. As late as 1982 the *Ilkley Gazette* reported that Dr Margaret Faull, a field officer with West Yorkshire County Archaeology, was stressing the urgency of housing the 'Ilkley Crosses' before the

manor of Otley included the berwicks (small manors or parts of manors) of Stubham, Middleton and Ilkley. In 1020 Archbishop Wulfstan's holding at Ilkley was six oxgangs, and at Middleton three oxgangs, an oxgang being the amount of land which could be ploughed by one team of oxen.

It is from ecclesiastical sources that we have the most information about Ilkley in the pre-Conquest Saxon period. The three exceptionally fine large carved crosses which can still be seen at Ilkley are amongst the most nationally important Anglo-Saxon sculptures which survive. It has been suggested they were associated with Wilfred, Bishop of Ripon and Hexham in the late seventh century (Leyland and Whitaker 1878, 285), but they are now thought to date from a slightly later period around 770-870 (Le Patourel 1968). The

winter arrived, and in 1983 they were at last placed under cover.

The crosses have no inscriptions but are ornamented with a variety of interlaced patterns, spirals, geometric shapes developing into animals and leafy shapes, and conventional animals with intertwined bodies (Romilly Allen 1884, 171). The shortest and most weathered shaft has a carving of a figure with a book on one panel, and animals inter-woven with scrolls on the others. These designs are probably the oldest of the tree cross shafts. Another shaft has stylised vine scroll patterns on two sides with intertwining animals, possibly hares or rabbits, and birds on the other panels and these carvings have remained sharp. The vine scroll pattern is somewhat reminiscent of the tree of life form. The tallest cross shaft is thought to be the latest, dating from around 850-70 (Le Patourel 1968, 7). One side is carved with four panels, each of which represents one of the four evangelists, a man for Matthew, a lion for St Mark, an ox for St Luke, and an eagle for St John, and is decorated with scroll and cable designs. Each carving covers a rectangular panel, clearly divided and with inter-woven decorative carvings not used elsewhere. On the opposite face are another four panels, one of which represents Christ and the others imaginary animals with inter-woven patterning. The other two sides of the shaft are decorated with circular scroll patterns and triple knots which represent the trinity. The cross head seen today does not belong to the shaft; the pieces having been joined together in 1914 after the crosspiece was recovered from Middleton Lodge.

25 *(Left) Three carved cross shafts inside All Saints Church.*

26 *(Right) The most weathered and shortest of the three carved cross shafts.*

27 *Four of the carved panels on one face of the largest cross shaft.*

The purpose of the crosses is unclear. They may have been erected to commemorate notable people buried at Ilkley or they may have been preaching crosses which served as the focus for Christian worship before the church was built. They are likely to have been painted originally, as similar stones of eighth and ninth century date at Monkwearmouth Priory (Sunderland) still have traces of colour adhering, and may have been decorated with glass or semi-precious stone in the eyes of the animals (Le Patourel 1968, 8 and Bailey 1996, 6-7). The mid-sized of the carved crosses at Ilkley may be by the sculptor who has become known as the 'Uredale Master'. Its paired animals and birds are cut in the style of sculpted stone at Masham, Cundall and Aldborough, and the plant scroll on this

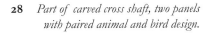

28 *Part of carved cross shaft, two panels with paired animal and bird design.*

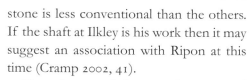

29 *(Right) Two former Roman carved alter stones re-cut to form window arches in an early church.*

30 *(Below) Roman altar stone with carving of a pitcher, one of the stones re-used as a window arch in an early church.*

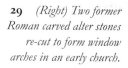

stone is less conventional than the others. If the shaft at Ilkley is his work then it may suggest an association with Ripon at this time (Cramp 2002, 41).

The existence of the carved crosses and fragments of grave slabs of the same date suggests there was a Saxon church at Ilkley. This was most likely built on or close to the site of the current parish church, at the south-west corner of the Roman fort. The Roman buildings which once stood there provided much material for the construction, and later re-building and alterations, of the church (Le Patourel 1968, 7). The abundance of Roman building stone meant the early church was likely to have been built of stone rather than timber. This re-use is illustrated by the discovery of two stones in the base of the tower which were once Roman altars. The larger is 3 feet 6 inches high and has a female figure carved on one side. The smaller, now broken in two, has a representation of a sacrificial pitcher and *patera* (shallow dish for drinking) carved on it in low relief. If either had an inscription these were removed when a large semi-circular cut was made on each of them, which indicates that the stone may have been used at the head of windows or doors and may have been part of the original Anglo-Saxon church before being re-used again in the 15th century when the tower was built (Le Patourel 1968, 8). Although the earliest architectural feature of the present church is a chiselled doorway dating to the early 13th century, it is possible the bases of the pillars on the north side are earlier than the pillars they carry and could be survivals of the Anglo-Saxon church (Le Patourel 1968, 17).

There were Saxon churches at neighbouring Addingham to the west and at Otley to the east. There is a record of the church and settlement at Addingham providing a refuge for Archbishop Wulfhere of York as he escaped from a Viking raid in 867, but Addingham succumbed to a later Viking raid in around 980 (Le Patourel 1968, 23). The physical remains strongly suggest there was a Saxon church at Ilkley as well, but there are no documentary records of this early church, or its history.

MEDIEVAL MANOR, CHURCH AND VILLAGE

The Domesday survey of 1085, as already noted, has two separate records of land holdings at Ilkley. One part is referred to amongst the holdings of the manor of Otley, which was held in 1085 by Thomas, Archbishop of York and included 'land at Ilecliue and Burley, Menston, Baildon, Esholt, Pool, Timble'. In the wapentake of Skyrack the archbishop's holdings included '1 carucate, 6 bovates at Ilkley' (p.1,912, 213). (A carucate was equivalent

31 *A stone effigy of a knight in armour holding a shield bearing the Middleton crest, Peter de Middleton who died in 1336. Once located a screened area on the south side of All Saints Church, St Nicholas chantry and moved in 1927 to niche made for it in the side chapel.*

32 *Detail of the effigy of Peter de Middleton, clad in chain mail, cross-legged, wearing spurs, feet resting on a lion. There is no inscription but the identification of the knight is based on an approximate dating of the style of dress and the documented wish of William Middleton in 1549 to be buried with his ancestor Peter de Middleton in Saint Nicholas's chantry.*

to around 120 acres and a bovate to around 15 acres.) The archbishop's holding had increased from the six oxgang he held in the early 10th century. A larger parcel of land at Ilkley is recorded amongst the very extensive holdings of William de Percy, who also held the nearby manors of Nessfield, Langbar, Stubham and Middleton, on the north side of the river. These manors all pre-date the Norman Conquest and lie within the two different wapentakes (ancient administrative divisions) of upper Skyrack, on the south side of the river, and upper Claro on the north side. There is scant information about the manor of Ilkley, although in William de Percy's holding there was a church with a priest and some three carucates of land which was cultivated before the Conquest and was then left uncultivated and is described as 'waste'.

'In Illicleia (Ilkley) Gamel had 3 carucates of land for geld, where 2 ploughs can be. Now William has it and it is waste. It was worth 20s. A church is there and a priest and pasturable woodland, 1 league in length and 4 furlongs in breadth. The whole manor has one league in length and 8 furlongs in width' (p.1,912, 259).

In 1251 Henry III granted Peter de Percy a charter for the free warren in all the demesne lands in Ilkley, together with the right to keep and kill all small beasts and birds such as hares, conies (rabbits), partridges, pheasants, quail and woodcock, for 20 marks (YAS MD59/8/4). The manors of Ilkley along with those on the opposite side of the river continued to belong to the Percy family although leased out. In 1284 Phillip Kyme held Ilkley from Percy and in return owed military service to him (Whitaker 1878, 278). In the 13th century the manor of Stubham was granted to Patrick Westwick and Peter de Middleton.

At the beginning of the 14th century Peter de Middleton was recorded as holding the manors of Stubham including Middleton, together with the manor of Draughton and Stokhill. Peter seems to have been an active knight, in 1333 raising troops to fight for Edward III in his battles with the Scots, and he may have been involved in the battle of Halidon near Berwick. He held various offices, including Sheriff of Yorkshire in 1335 (Le Patourel 968, 11). There is a recumbent effigy of a knight in armour, a memorial to Peter de Myddleton, identified by the Middleton family crest on the shield, dating from about 1336. It lies in Ilkley parish church, All Saints, and indicates the local importance of Middleton, as lord of the manor at Stubham and Middleton before the family came to be lords of the manor at Ilkley. They continued to hold the manor at Stubham and Middleton, together with other hamlets on the south side of the river Wharfe (YAS MD59/14/Midd/56) and other land, through to the 15th century.

The history of landholding in the locality is a changing tapestry which cannot be shown here in full detail. The manor of Ilkley was already divided at the beginning of the medieval period, and further subdivision, unification and changing ownership was to take place. In the 14th century it seems to have been divided up, with Robert de Percy, the Abbott of Sawley and the Abbot of Fountains Abbey holding portions. In the 15th century the manor became part of the holdings of the Plesynton, or Plesyington, family. A surviving document from 1457 shows

33 *Middleton family crest (Argent fretty sable with a canton in the second) displayed in All Saints Church.*

that Isabel Plesyington appointed Thomas Clapham of Beamsley steward of the manor of Ilkley and granted him the annual rent of 40 shillings (YAS MD59/12/74). Isabel, the daughter of John de Plesyington, married John Fraunceys (Page 1935, 112-19) and in 1461 they were granted the manor of Ilkley, with lands, meadows, moor, wood and rents in Ilkley, Addingham, Austby, Nessfield and Wheatley, by William Vavasour and William Boure (YAS MD59/12/52). In 1464 William Plesyington and his son conferred the manor of Ilkley on William Middleton of Stubham for the sum of 50 marks (YAS MD59/21/pack4/25) and later, in the 16th century, the manor of Ilkley came to be held by the Meryng family. In 1514 Robert Meryng is recorded as holding the manor, and in 1552 it was again granted to the Middletons of Stubham, this time John Middleton. Francis Meryng also sold his lease of the church and rectory of

Ilkley, owned by the priory of Hexham since 1406, for the sum of £706 13s. 4d. (YAS MD59/12/2), the priory of Hexham retaining ownership of the church until 1541. The Middleton family retained the manor of Ilkley until 1763. Their principal residence was not at Stubham, Middleton or Ilkley, but at Stockeld (near Wetherby) and they came to be known as Middleton of Stockeld. After 1763 the manor was not inherited directly by a Middleton, but by a relation who under the terms of inheritance was obliged to take on the

name of Middleton, and so it continued until financial difficulties led to land sales, eventually of the entire manor in the later part of the 19th century.

In 1553 the medieval manor of Ilkley was described as a manor with 40 messuages, one watermill, 300 acres of meadow, 300 acres of pasture, 100 acres of woodland, 4,000 acres of moor, 40 shillings of rents and free fishing (YAS MD59/12/48). The farmed land seems to have operated with a two-field system rather than the more usual medieval three-field system. This

34 *A 19th-century photograph of the old bridge across the Wharfe at Ilkley.*

arrangement probably developed because of the constraints of topography, with one open-field system to the west and one to the east of the village. Medieval open fields were made up of a series of long individual strips measured in furlongs (furrow long). Over time holdings of individual strips were often consolidated into larger groups and later enclosed as fields.

At the time of the Domesday Survey there was probably some form of settlement at Ilkley, but all that is known with certainty is that there was a church and priest. A market charter was granted to Ilkley in 1252, indicating that the village may have begun to develop into a small market town, although the grant of a charter did not necessarily mean that much trading took place. It was in effect a licence to hold a market, and what actually happened would depend on how interested the lord of the manor was in developing the commercial activity of the town. If markets were held at Ilkley then temporary wooden market stalls must have been used, leaving no trace, since there is no indication of the specific area which was used. No records of a market square or market cross have survived.

Traffic travelling north to south would probably have crossed the Wharfe at the ford which had been in use since Roman times, if not before. It may have included salt on its way from Cheshire via Manchester to Yorkshire, but nothing survives at Ilkley to indicate this particular trade. Transport across the river would have been improved in the 15th century when Richard Brame of Adel left the sum of 13s. 4d. in his will of 1446 for the purpose of building a bridge called 'Ilklay Brig'. This bridge was

the first of a number, as in 1638 'a newly built bridge' was swept away by a flood, and parish registers at Otley note that the floods of 1673 destroyed several bridges, including the one at Ilkley. The present packhorse bridge probably dates from this period and has three arches, which form quite a steeply graded crossing. It is now closed to all motor traffic, which crosses the river further downstream.

It would seem that the site of the Roman fort became established as the core of the medieval village. The church was re-built or re-modelled in the 14th century but still incorporates an earlier, 13th-century, door at the south entrance. Although the church has undergone later rebuilding, the present north wall dates from the 14th century and a tower was added in the 15th century. Investigations have also revealed a substantial foundation, possibly for an early west wall. Much of the stone used in this foundation was re-used from the Roman period. The majority of the present church, although retaining the dimensions and style of the late medieval building, dates from 1860-1 (Le Patourel 1968, 7) but incorporates re-used Roman stones.

An early manor house may have been built next to the church, but the earliest

35 *(Inset) Early 13th-century dog tooth moulding on the church doorway at All Saints Church.*

36 *All Saints Church tower.*

37 *'The Castle', now the Manor House Museum, built on the site of the Roman fort.*

date for the remains of medieval buildings here is the 13th or 14th century. Stone buildings within the site of the fort re-used foundations of Roman buildings and Roman building stone. Stretches of the fort wall may have been used as a precinct boundary. The earliest part of the building which now stands to the north-west of the church probably dates from the 14th century. It is now known as the 'Manor House' and houses a museum, but has formerly been known as the 'Castle'. Foundations of a medieval building and medieval pottery were located in the north-west corner of the former fort during excavations in 1920-1 and may have been part of a separate building range (WYAS 1987, 1992). Remains discovered here include a stone latrine, indicating a building of some status, located to north of the present museum. Most of this group was

demolished during a later rebuilding of the main structure, the 'Castle', in the 16th century. Characteristically, Roman squared blocks are evident in the building. Its name may come from its location, on the raised area of the former fort above the river, rather than any from defensive qualities it may have possessed. It is not a bastle or 'strong' house, built with defence in mind.

By 1378 there is known to have been one inn at Ilkley, where Henry Spenser was the 'hostiler'. This could have been on the site of the *Rose and Crown*, located on Church Street opposite the church, which has a long history as a coaching inn, although alternative claims could be made. The medieval village mainly comprised farm houses and cottages clustered near the site of the former fort. These were mostly single-storey buildings with stone walls utilising the freely available Roman building materials, with thatched roofs. The main east-west street of the village would have run along the line of the present Church Street, from which a path running south at right angles was one of the routes to the common pastures of Ilkley Moor (along the line of the present Brook Street and Cowpasture Lane). Another lane, Green Lane (now The Grove), ran to the south of, and parallel with, Church Street. This arrangement, which can be seen in the layout of the modern town, changed little for several hundred years, until significant development took place in the mid-19th century.

A stream (now culverted) flowed down from the moorland, cutting the steep valley of Mill Ghyll and continuing down what is now Brook Street to the Wharfe. A path led up Mill Ghyll from the village to the manorial corn mill, which is first recorded in the early 13th century. While agriculture was the main stay of the local economy, a textile mill for making woollen cloth is known to have been working here. This fulling mill is assumed to have been located in Mill Ghyll, near the corn mill, and the 1378 Poll Tax records two walkers or fullers, called Henry and William, working at Ilkley. This mill seems to have been later converted to work corn, for in 1631 Henry Currer, Sir Peter Middleton's bailiff, was leased the two corn mills, the watercourses and the mill houses (YAS MD59/12/29). Later maps show the

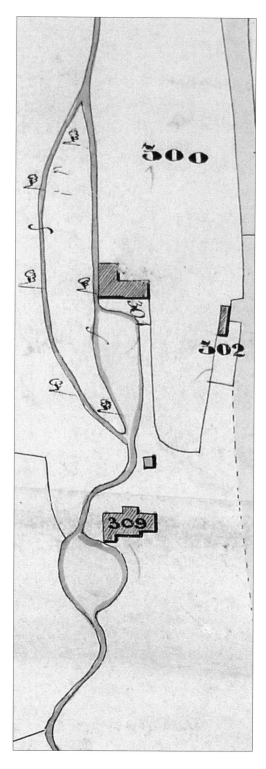

38 *Extract from Tithe Map, 1847, showing two mills on Mill Ghyll on the hillside directly above Ilkley.*

39 *Water Mill in Mill Ghyll, photographed c.1870.*

two corn mills on the Ghyll, Low Mill and Upper Mill, powered by water from a mill race where The Tarn was later constructed.

Other trades represented in the 1378 Poll Tax list for Ilkley show William Tailor was a tailor and Robert Baynbrig a souter or shoemaker. The records show that there were 25 married couples and 18 single people in total in the manor of Ilkley; at Middleton there were 13 married couples and 23 single people, and there were 17 married couples at Nessfield as well as 16 single people. The figures for baptisms and deaths in the parish records for the period between 1600 and 1700 illustrate a relatively unchanged population and reflect the relatively slow rate of change in the character of the village from the medieval period to modern times.

A description of Ilkley in a topographic guide to Wharfedale in 1813 gives some indication of its unchanging character and so the description might also have been appropriate for the medieval village.

> The village is very compact, consisting of a main street, where the houses join each other, except on one side where this is the church and its yard and there are two lateral (houses) which proceed from it at right angles, one north and the other south. An Antiquary easily sees an air of antiquity about the houses, many of them having being built above a hundred years. On the south, the Common called Rombalds Moor occupies the summits of the overhanging mountains.
>
> (Anon 1813, 22).

Four

THE TOWNSHIP WITHIN THE MIDDLETON ESTATE IN THE 16TH TO EARLY 19TH CENTURIES

Since the township of Ilkley was a part of the Middleton estate for many centuries the family's management was a primary influence over the path taken for the development of the town. The Middletons' methods and their attitudes to estate management, the decisions they took, their use of finance, their religion and the impact of their family history have all had a major role to play in the direction of the township and the development of Ilkley.

The Middleton family were Catholics who retained and practised their faith after the Reformation and later, in 1825, a Catholic chapel was built at Middleton. In 1634 Sir Peter Middleton had to appear before commissioners to answer for the recusancy of his wife, Mary, but although they were authorised to forfeit lands and goods, Middleton must have paid money instead and the sheriff did not trouble them further at this time (YAS MD59/25/42a). It seems likely that the family did not play a particularly significant part in the Civil War as there is scant record of them at this time. After the Civil War in 1652 they were amongst the gentry whom the Commonwealth Parliament listed as dissident recusants. It passed a bill

to allow their estates to be sold, with the proceeds going for the use of the navy (JHC 1651-60, 156-7), but it seems that, although rents from the Middleton estates were collected on behalf of the Commonwealth, the estates were not sold off, and at the time of the Restoration were restored to the Middletons. There are records of the manor of Ilkley being mortgaged in 1674 and 1677 (YAS MD59/20/Misc/31 and 32) but a century later, when William Middleton died in 1763, the estates were in better financial state and debts which resulted from sequestration during the Commonwealth were paid off. The annual rental income from the Middleton estate in 1762, just before William's death, was: Ilkley £230, Askwith £60, Austby and Nessfield £153, Middleton £561, Stockeld £412, Sicklinghall Spofforth and Follifoot £31, Habton £316 and North Duffield £916, amounting to a total of £2,700 (Collyer 1885).

At the death of William Middleton in 1763 there was no male heir, but William had made legal provision to ensure the name and arms of the Middleton family would continue. The inheritance, through the female line, went to the second son of

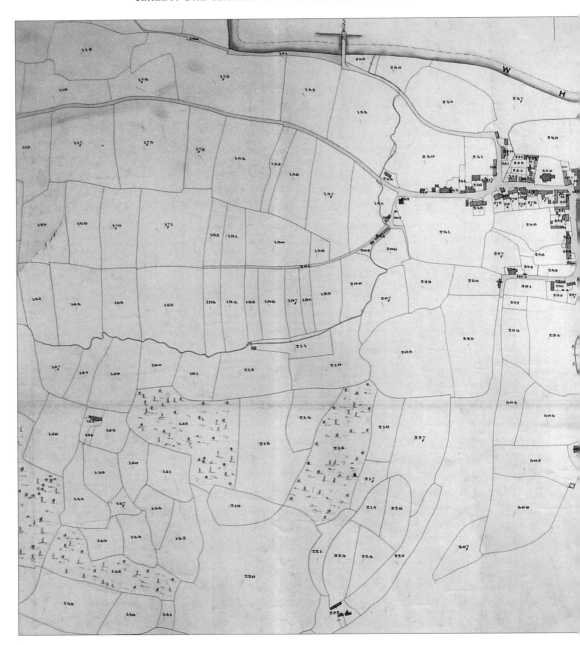

40 *Part of Ilkley Tithe Map, 1847.*

his nephew William Haggerston, also called William, and specified that the boy would take on the Middleton name as his own and the arms and estate would be retained in the future. The estates were held in trust until William came of age, in 1782, when he took control of his estates and married in the same year. He and his wife Clara

46

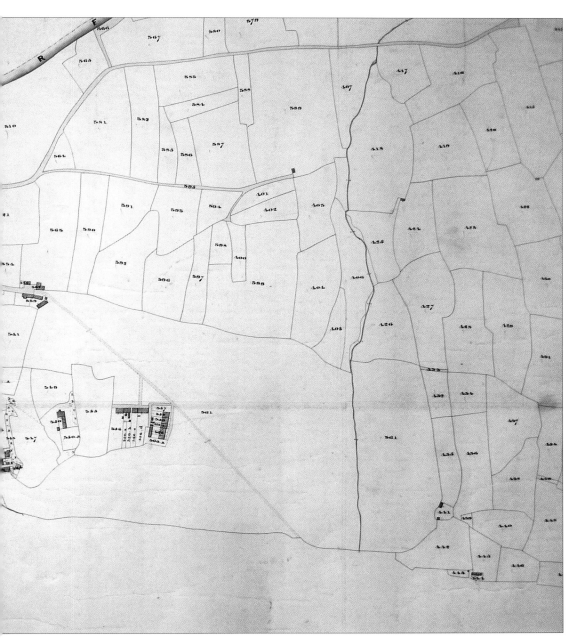

initially lived at Myddleton Lodge before moving to the main residence at Stockeld Lodge near Wetherby (Carpenter 1999, 10). The running of the estate at Ilkley appears to have continued undisturbed for ten years until an accusation of adultery by Clara with the groom at Stockeld, John Rose, led to very drawn out divorce proceedings. The case was to become the most expensive and longest marital law suit of the century (Stone 1990). William Middleton moved his establishment back to Myddleton Lodge and remained there for the rest of his life (Captenter 1999, 41). Part of the Middleton estate at Duffield was sold off to cover the legal costs but the main consequence of the divorce for the estate was not financial but the fact that William Middleton did not attend to its development or improvement.

THE ESTATE: AGRICULTURE

Alterations to the medieval open-field system occurred over time with the two open fields to the east and to the west of the town enclosed and some additional land brought into cultivation. These 'intakes' are so called because they were created beyond the extent of land cultivated in the medieval open fields. In 1623 Sir Peter Middleton sold Lawson intake, a parcel of improved land, and a barn to a glover, William Lawson of Gybfield, and other intake fields were created along the bottom of the moor above Heber's Ghyll and Hollin Hall Woods, as the Tithe Map of 1847 and the first Ordnance Survey map of 1851 show. However, no additional land at Ilkley was enclosed during the 18th century, when many other landowners were improving their land and increasing the amount of land under cultivation. William Middleton did not enclose either Middleton or Ilkley Moors, preserving them as woodlands and open moor for hunting game. Enclosure of valuable common land at Cow Pasture was not carried out until 1858. Farm leases show that responsibilities to maintain the land were laid down for farmers. Twelve wagon-loads of manure and two cauldrons of burned lime were required for each acre, for example, but there was little incentive for

41 *A pencil drawing by William Henty, c.1860, looking south at Ilkley and Ben Rhydding from the north side of the river Wharfe, the rural character of the village still apparent and Hangingstone rocks (the Cow and Calf) visible on the skyline.*

tenants to invest more effort or expense in improvements since the tenancies were only held for the term of a year. In contrast, leases for the term of 21 years were common in the 17th century in Ilkley.

These factors meant that very little alteration was made to the land and the pattern of the landscape in fields and

acres were meadow and pasture, and not mapped were 152 acres of woodland and 2,000 acres of uncultivated waste, or moorland (Long 2005, 5). The total amount of farmed acreage which was arable or pasture appears to have reduced between 1793 and 1847, not because of urban expansion but because there were few attempts to improve the moorland, or 'waste', and woodland.

FROM TOWNSHIP INTO TOWN

A watercolour of Ilkley from the river Wharfe painted by Thomas Girtin in 1801 shows the view from a point on the north bank of the river looking south. The Manor House and, behind it, the tower of Ilkley parish church can be seen on the raised platform of the former Roman fort to the left of the picture. One of the narrow valleys with a beck running from the moorland to the river Wharfe is shown with a farmhouse to the right of the picture. The picture may be a romantic vision of Ilkley at the very beginning of the 19th century, but it does show how, at that time, there was a complete absence of any urban development in the town, and it amply demonstrates that, despite its ancient foundations, its character today is a creation of the 19th and 20th centuries. The strong influence of the landscape on the setting of the town is apparent in the picture and remains true today.

farms survived from the 17th into the 19th century. A survey of agriculture in West Yorkshire in 1793 records 1,800 acres of enclosed land in the township of Ilkley and 1,379 acres of potatoes and pasture, 371 acres of arable land, 2,400 acres of moor and woodland, 50 acres of woods, and 95 acres of fallow or turnips and potatoes (Brown 1793, 76). The earliest surviving map of Ilkley is the Tithe Map of 1847, and the Tithe Apportion lists the owners of each parcel of land depicted on it. The map shows that 404 acres out of a total of 3,961 acres were under arable cultivation, 1,192

In the 17th and 18th centuries Ilkley was a small township within a largely agricultural parish. An impression of the types of house in the parish can be gained from the Hearth Tax returns from 1672.

42 *Manor House, c.1866, in poor state of repair with a hole in the roof.*

well into the 19th century. The church of All Saints stood at the core of the settlement. In the glebe terrier of 1770 a tithe barn was described as standing on the north side of the church yard, but it no longer survives (Long 2005, 2). The substantial house standing next to the church was rebuilt in the 16th century and a record survives from 1631, when it was called the 'Castle' and was leased with an orchard by Peter Middleton of Stockeld to Anne Longfellow of Ilkley, widow, for 21 years at a token annual rent of one penny (YAS MD 59/12/16). It is not identifiable as a single large house in the Hearth Tax returns in 1672 but could by then have been sub-divided, as it was known to be in the 19th century. An early photograph dating from about 1866 shows the building in a very poor state of repair with a large hole in its roof. The house has since been extensively restored and is now the Manor House Museum.

They show great variation, with over 100 single-hearth houses (the homes of the poorest householders), including an estimated 40 who were too poor to pay the tax. There were 25 larger houses with two hearths, 14 with three hearths, three with four hearths, four with five hearths and only one eight-hearth house, Wheatley Hall. The residences belonging to the local landowners were by far the largest houses, Middleton Lodge with 21 hearths and Low Hall (on Rupert Road) with 18 (Pickles 2002, 11).

The extents of the township were probably close to those of its medieval predecessor and changed very little until

The buildings of the township were concentrated around the church to each side of the main streets, Church Street running east to west, and Brook Street running north to south. In amongst these domestic dwellings would have been public houses and shops. The Tithe Map shows three public houses and three shops located on Church Street. In 1838

43 *A sketch of Ilkley, looking north down Brook Street, taken from a lithograph by the Rev. Thomas Kilby, c.1835, showing the rural nature of the village.*

44 *A sketch, looking south up Brook Street, c.1835.*

there were around twelve houses with slate roofs, the remainder being low cottages with thatched roofs on Brook Street described as 'lying along one of the streams which ran into the river below the ancient church' (Speight 1900, 202). More prosaically, 'Brook Street with a brook running down the middle of the street was lined by a choice collection of middens' (Collyer 1885).

Very little remains of the medieval or early modern buildings, although some significant older buildings do survive within the core of the village. The Box Tree Restaurant is a surviving early 18th-century farmhouse on the south side of Church Street, and the *Albert Inn*, on the north side of the street, has a date stone

of 1709. An earlier surviving building is the Old Grammar School, constructed in 1635-6 and located to the west of the core of the old village on Skipton Road. Records of a schoolmaster date from 1575 and an endowment was established in 1603 by Sir Thomas Fairfax of Denton and Sir Mawger Vavasour of Weston from which a salary for a schoolmaster was to be paid. Before the purpose-built school was constructed the church may have been used (Le Patourel 1968, 26). The school was built with donations from parishioners, including Reginald Heber of Hollin Hall. Since the building ceased to be used as a school in 1872 it has been a shoemakers shop, and a chapel used by the Christian Brethren. It is now a shop selling antique silver.

45 *An early 18th-century farmhouse on Church Street, photographed c.1880s (now the Box Tree Restaurant).*

46   *The lowest building to the left of the picture, with mullioned windows, once a dairy (now a public house, The Albert) has a date stone of 1709.*

47   *Old Grammar School, constructed 1635-6.*

48 *The Old Grammar School constructed 1635-6, with the schoolmaster and pupils in* c.*1870.*

PEOPLE AND WORK

The early modern township was very agricultural in character, with farm houses and stables located in the main streets and on Green Lane which ran parallel and to the south of Church Street. This is now The Grove but was then described as a 'narrow leafy track' (Collyer 1885). Hartley's farmhouse and an old thatched cottage were the only buildings on Green Lane, although the stack yard of a farm on Green Lane was located at the corner with Brook Street. There would have been a smithy somewhere in the village. An apprentice's indenture from 1598 survives showing that the blacksmith Thomas Shaw of Ilkley took on Walter Pollard of Tranmyre, Otley as his apprentice for seven years. The Tithe Map shows a smith's shop centrally located, near the crossroads of the main streets, in

1847 when it was leased to Samson Spike. There were also two corn mills and some cottages on the lower part of Mill Gill and cottages further to the east (in what is now Station Road).

The parish registers for the first half of the 18th century show the town's population to have been mainly yeomen farmers and labourers with a few men plying other essential trades such as carpenter, tailor, shoemaker, butcher, brewer and linen weaver. The majority of the inhabitants of Ilkley were engaged in occupations either directly or indirectly related to agriculture. Tanning, often a spin-off trade from agriculture, was carried out at Nessfield and Ilkley. Edward Beanlands, tanner of Ilkley, died in 1689 leaving a significant estate. The only more 'exotic' trader seems to be another Beanlands, John, who in 1725 was a tobacconist.

49   *Thatched cottage, boot and shoe maker in Brook Street, c.1869.*

50   *Hangingstone Quarry, at the Cow and Calf rocks looking across the modern town of Ilkley.*

Stone was quarried from the many various places where it outcrops on Ilkley Moor and disused quarries are a part of the modern landscape so, not surprisingly, another trade occupying several villagers was stonemason and quarryman. A major quarry site was at Hanging Stones ('The Cow and Calf'), stone quarried here being brought down from the moor along Cow Pasture Road which was then a path running through the common pastures. Stone was also used to manufacture millstones, abandoned examples of which still lie in the Panorama Woods.

Elsewhere on the moors other natural resources were exploited. An erratic glacial deposition including limestone boulders, at Lanshaw on Rombald's Moor, is known to have been quarried for lime for bleaching textiles and for agricultural purposes. The area is now marked on the Ordnance Survey map as 'Lanshaw delves'. The lime may have been processed in the old limekilns on the nearby hillside above the White Wells. These kilns, no longer surviving, are mentioned in passing by Thomas Short in 1734.

From the later part of the 18th century and into the 19th century, industrial development was taking place on a significant scale in nearby towns and villages, but in Ilkley William Middleton showed only a slight interest and made limited efforts in this field. Certainly, he displayed none of the enthusiasm of the age for this new activity. He made a survey of his estates for coal in 1792 but this led to no further action. Unsurprisingly, during the 17th and 18th centuries there was a migration of population from the parish of Ilkley, probably to the

51 *Millstone in Panorama Woods.*

woollen manufacturing towns of Leeds and Bradford.

Worsted was being traded in Leeds, Skipton and Keighley from the very beginning of the 18th century, and the textile trade began to figure as a significant occupation in West Yorkshire in this period. In Wharfedale both cotton and woollen manufacture were to be strongly represented, although at the beginning of the 18th century wool was the predominant industry, mostly carried on at the domestic level. The preamble to the local Turnpike

Act of 1755 listed Addingham, Ilkley and Kildwick as places where woollen manufacture was carried out, and stated that 'There are three or four hundred weavers or more and great numbers of inferior workmen employed under them. The families weave usually on their own accounts and dispose of their goods in Halifax or Colne.' At Ilkley, at the beginning of the century, John Clough is recorded as a linen weaver in the parish registers for 1718. Between 1745 and 1750 the parish registers record more than a dozen different weavers and wool-combers living at Ilkley, one of whom, Nathan Hoyl, was both an innkeeper and wool-comber.

More people may have been 'invisibly' occupied in the cloth processing and manufacture trade but only the occupations of heads of household were noted in the parish registers. Later census returns show many examples of a head of the household employed in agriculture, while wives and younger family members were occupied in cloth processing. Spinning and weaving took place in domestic settings before textile mills were built and domestic production carried on for a time alongside that of the mills, so more of the population of Ilkley may have been occupied in the textile trade than is shown by the parish registers.

The manufacture of textiles was predominant in the development of many other towns in West Yorkshire and as the 18th century progressed the parish registers show a significant increase in those occupied in the industry within the parish of Ilkley. Ilkley, however, provides a striking contrast not only with the larger towns but with the comparable smaller nearby settlements at Burley in Wharfedale to the east and Addingham to the west. In Burley there were four mills employing 360 people in the 18th century, including Greenholme Mill, one of the largest cotton mills to be built in Yorkshire; the neighbouring town of Addingham became a centre of production of both woollen worsted and cotton calico manufacture. It included a very large mill, Low Mill, founded in 1789 by John Cunliffe of Ilkley and John Cockshott, initially intended to be a cotton mill but altered for worsted and then later, in 1824, re-equipped for cotton (Ingle 1997, 218). The disparity between Ilkley and its neighbouring towns increased during the 19th century and Pigots Directory in 1834 listed four Cotton Spinners and Manufacturers and five Worsted Spinners and Manufacturers for Addingham but none for Ilkley.

Ilkley's first and only textile mill was built in 1786 on the upper reaches of Mill Gill 'for manufacture of cotton wool into yarn or for spinning of manufacturing linen, wool or worsted' (YAS MD59/25/46). It used a 'water-frame' invented in 1769 by Richard Arkwright, which was first used to spin cotton in Lancashire but was applied for wool, and greatly speeded up the pace of spinning either yarn. Thus, Ilkley dipped a toe in the water of the industrial revolution at a time when new machinery was inducing widespread change in other towns in the region. Thomas Hauxworth of Ilkley, gentleman, Jonathan Curtis of Bingley, a worstedman, and Joseph Hartley of Keighley, an engineer, leased land called Kilner Croft for the mill from William Middleton, the lord of the manor. The lease stated that the mill was to be '45 feet in length, 31 feet in breadth and 25 feet from the ground', and that no more than 30 people might be employed there. It included a warehouse, offices and a counting house in addition to the mill (Ingle 1997, 400). Kilner Croft was powered by the water of Mill Ghyll and was upstream of two working corn mills. The lord of the manor reiterated the ancient right whereby all his tenant's corn had to be ground at his corn mills and the deeds relating to the construction of the textile mill explicitly stated that the new mill could not be used for grinding corn. However, he did agree to divert some of the water from the streams serving the corn mills so that water could power the new mill wheel then be redirected back to power the corn mills.

The mill may have been used to spin both wool and cotton at the start, but Curtis, the worsted spinner, sold off his part in 1797 when in financial difficulties and the mill seems to have been used exclusively for cotton thereafter (Ingle 1997, 400). It was still in use in the 1830s but the exact date at which cotton mill production ceased is not known. By 1850 the site was described by the naturalist Charles Waterton as 'the shell of an old factory on the edge of Ilkley Moor, now used as three very indifferent cottages' (Waterton 1955, 116). The 1847-8 Ordnance Survey map marks Moor Cottage above the corn mills on Mill Gill, and this became the site of Wells House Hydro in 1856 (now converted to apartments). The domestic scale of textile working is represented by a surviving row of early 19th-century handloom weaver's cottages to the rear of Brook Street. This short row of three cottages had a communal workshop running through the length of the first floor. Meetings of Methodists were held here before a church was built.

The small textile mill established at Ilkley employed a small number of workers, but most textile workers were scattered about the parish, the trade complementing their agricultural work, so the industry had very little impact on the development of the township. Middleton's lack of enthusiasm for either industrial development or agricultural improvement meant the income from the estates was not increased during this period, which contributed to later financial problems for the estate. But his philosophy also ensured the township of Ilkley and the surrounding countryside were not exploited for anything other than the hunting pursuits of the gentry, which meant that the area was able to retain the natural advantages of pure air and beautiful moorland scenery. In these qualities lay a quite different line of development for the future.

Five

THE WATERS OF ILKLEY

A combination of its attractive setting and abundance of pure natural spring water and bracing air provided the basis for the development of the township into a fashionable and popular spa resort by the end of the 18th century. From the middle of that century improvements to the national road network had enabled the upper and middle classes to endure what were still long and uncomfortable journeys to rural spa towns like Ilkley in pursuit of health and the enjoyment of rural pleasures. Ilkley was well placed in this respect, being on the stage carriage routes from Leeds to Skipton and York to the Lake District. Ilkley followed the pattern of the older rural spa towns in England, like Bath, Buxton, Scarborough and Tunbridge Wells, the spa being developed and promoted initially by a local landowner often with the aid of a physician or apothecary. At

52 *White Wells on Ilkley Moor.*

Ilkley, principal landowner and lord of the manor William Middleton erected the White Wells Bath House in 1699 at the site of a natural spring, and 'taking the waters' there helped pave the way for what became a 'hydropathic boom' in the 19th century. The popularity of hydrotherapy accounted for much of Ilkley's growth into a town and this growth was planned and controlled partly with the intention of creating a town attractive to visitors.

SPA WATER: THE ILKLEY FOUNTAIN

Ilkley's spa waters first attained some popularity at the beginning of the 18th century despite the town itself not being very attractive to visitors. Dr Richardson, writing in the preface of Thomas Hearne's 1710-12 edition of *Leland's Itinerary*, describes Ilkley as 'a very mean place and is equally dirty and insignificant, and chiefly famous for a cold well which has done very remarkable cures in scrofulous cases by bathing and in the drinking of it'. Whitaker uses the same unflattering adjectives to describe Ilkley in his *History of Manchester* in 1773. The town continued to get a bad press and in the 1820s was described as 'one of the most rustic, inaccessible and primitive little places in the country. The streets are full of ruts and holes and lined by stinking refuse.'

The spa water at Ilkley comes from springs high above the town on Rombald's Moor. A bath house was first erected at White Wells in 1699, 'about a furlong below the original spring, which was brought down in stone pipes' (Short 1734). The waters at White Wells were also known

as the Ilkley Fountain. Thomas Short, a Scottish physician practising in Sheffield who wrote the *Natural, experimental and medicinal history of the mineral waters of Derbyshire, Lincolnshire and Yorkshire* in 1734, gives a rich account of Ilkley's waters, which he describes as 'Ichley-Spaw', springing 'out of the middle of a mountain, a mile high, and consists mainly of limestone and free stone. The water is very clear, brisk and sparkling; has no taste, colour nor smell different from common water, is of the same weight. Its bason and course are of no other dye than of a common spring ... The water is first whitish, then blackish purple, with solution of silver.' The healing properties attributed to the water were thought to derive from its coldness and purity.

During the century after this description was written, visiting Ilkley to take the waters become an established and popular activity, although the town never competed seriously with the nearby, long established and more fashionable, Harrogate spa. It seems that visitors came to Ilkley before any facilities had been developed, a national gazetteer dated 1795 describing the waters as have been well frequented for the past 50 years (Paterson 1795, 146). The attraction of the waters were enhanced in 1791, when two 'commodious stone baths and sitting rooms' were constructed at White Wells (*Leeds Intelligencer* 26 April 1791). Middleton is commended for having 'spent a considerable amount' in building the baths and dressing rooms and on providing 'every convenience for a bathing place of this sort' (Shaw 1830, 75). These baths were at first open to the sky, and the Spartan character of taking the waters

53 *The Charity Bath at White Wells.*

was regarded as part of the cure. In 1829 Middleton also erected a Charity Bath for the poor (Hembry 1997, 173); it lies just to the west of White Wells and has now been converted to a public toilet.

Granville, a physician who visited and wrote two volumes about the spas in Germany and England, reported that several local doctors, including Dr Spence, surgeon of Ilkley, Dr Mossman, Mr Moorhouse, surgeon of Skipton, and Dr Hunter of Leeds, one of the founders of the Leeds University School of Medicine in 1831, recommended their patients to take treatments at the Ilkley Fountain (Granville 1841, 387). In 1819 Hunter embroidered the attraction of the spring water at White Wells by associating it with the Roman altar found at Ilkley. The supposed Roman connection has persisted to this day, but there is no evidence to suggest the White Wells spring has any ancient association.

The description of Ilkley in Pigot's directory in 1829 is concise and indicates that the predominant reason for visiting the town was to sample the spa waters: 'Ilkley, a village, in the parish of its name, in the wapentake of Skyrack and Claro, is six miles from Otley, much frequented in the summer for the benefit of its cold spring,

55 *Looking west to White Wells and the upper tarn.*

54 *Spring water well at the rear of White Wells.*

which issues from the sides of a high hill overlooking the village, and the bath is deemed highly salutary in relaxed and scorbutic cases. The population is about 500.' One of the reasons for the success of Ilkley as a spa was its setting, one of great natural beauty, with monumental rocks outcropping on Rombald's Moor above the town. The visual impact of White Wells, perched on the steep hillside above Ilkley, is conveyed in Granville's description of his visit in 1841.

As we passed Burley (in Wharfedale) the glaring white house of Ilkley Fountain, stuck, as it were, midway on the steep ascent of the Rumbold Moor, betokened our immediate approach to the Spa village … The effect produced by the sight of that single and insulated building, within which thousands have been known to quaff the pure stream that gives health, and which to a superficial observer seems almost unapproachable, is one of that class

which can hardly be expressed in words. As the carriage wound up the road, the humble fabric appeared and disappeared alternately, screened by the tufty and woody scene which spreads from the margin of the river as to the foot of the hilly range, and it creeps up its precipitous side to a considerable height. It would be the most attractive object for the moment, were not the attention of the beholder, while scanning the many beauties of this region, called to a mass of rocks … which stands as if perched on the summit of a point or headland of the Rumbold Moor … known as the Cow and Calf.

(Granville 1841, 383)

Although Ilkley was 'purely and intrinsically a rural retreat' (Granville 1841, 385) with a relatively small population, it was nevertheless considered the 'Arcadia or Malvern of the northern counties' (Granville 1841, 385). A spa visit came to be regarded as a necessity among the 'higher grades of factory society at Halifax, Bradford, Leeds, Huddersfield, Wakefield,

Sheffield or even Manchester'. However, Granville noted that it would not be fashionable to stay more than a fortnight or a month in the region and Ilkley was still unknown south of Yorkshire and Lancashire, and he described it as 'a terra incognita' in Middlesex.

By 1829 over thirty lodging houses catered for visitors to the spa, and in 1831 the census recorded that nearly a quarter of the population were visitors to the town. An impression of visiting at this time is given by a contemporary account which describes Ilkley as 'a little old and ragged village, but of considerable note on account of the wells or springs most rare for their purity and coolness and for some medicinal qualities. Here were found many genteel people crowding the low and thatched cottages and submitting to all sorts of romantic inconveniences

for the sake of their health.' (Colton 1835, 166) A visitor's guide of 1829 also listed six boarding houses and three inns (Guide 1829). One of these, the *Lister Arms*, was built on Church Street in 1825. Granville describes the lodging houses in Ilkley as 'sufficiently comfortable and some afford the convenience of boarding at a very moderate charge. Water is of the purest sort. Vegetables are in abundance and milk is excellent, owing to the green pasturage and water fields near to the river. The air is pure and elastic.' (1841, 384) A carriage and donkey hiring service was established at Bridge Street and in 1829 a total of five such transport services were advertised in a visitor's guide, using donkeys, asses or mules to transport visitors from the town up the steep track to the spring water at White Wells.

56 *Visitors at Hangingstones, the 'Cow and Calf', c.1890s.*

57 *Butterfield's donkey stand.*

At this time there were two baths, 'one for male and another for female patients. They are both open above, occupying a round area, three feet deep, surrounded by a wall. Over a centre room, placed between the two baths, there is a dressing room, but all this arrangement is quite in the rough, and the whole building looks very much like one of those stone built shelters or houses of recovery one meets on the Alps.' (Granville 1841, 386) The 'healing waters' were described as bursting from the rocky mountain side at the rate of sixty gallons per minute; the temperature 47 degrees Fahrenheit. It is brilliant, limpid and crystal-like; but its taste disappointed me, being, like the water in Malvern, which it resembles in other respects, neither sharp or very sapid. From two to three pints of it are generally drunk by the visitors, who take long and fatiguing walks, round about the mazes of these hills, between the several doses of water. But the principal use of the waters is in bathing, or still more for the application of the douche to any diseased parts of the body or limb.'

HYDROTHERAPY BOOM TOWN

The healing properties of the spa water become widely known and Ilkley was already an established spa village when the medical system of hydrotherapy was introduced and popularised in the 18th century. Hydrotherapy, or 'scientific water cure', consisted of systems of bathing and drinking spa waters in a variety of austere conditions. It formed an entire medical system, excluding all other forms of treatment, and was based on the internal and external application of water (Dupree 2007). It differed from the long-held belief in the curative properties of 'taking the waters' inasmuch as it was not through the minerals in the water that a cure might be effected, but through the action of water itself.

Hydrotherapy was devised in Gräfenberg, Austria (now Jesenik in the Czech Republic) in the 1820s, when a farmer, Vincent Priessnitz, developed the cure empirically, by using first his livestock and then his willing neighbours as subjects. He later established a water cure centre in the Silesian Alps and his medical system, based on the restorative effects of water and the benefits of healthy air and a plain diet, contrasted strongly with the medical practice of the time when treatments were predominantly emetics, bleeding and leeching (Dupree 2007). There is some rivalry between the spa towns of Ilkley and Malvern as to which was the first to establish hydrotherapy in England. In 1841, the year before Dr James Wilson introduced hydrotherapy to Malvern, Granville saw Ilkley as a future English Gräfenberg (Hembry 1997, 173). Dr Rischanek from Silesia, a student of Priessnitz in Gräfenberg, was practicing hydrotherapy in Ilkley in 1843 (Constantine 1884, 12) and the purpose-built hydrotherapy establishment at Ben Rhydding was opened in 1844, a year before Dr Wilson opened a purpose-built

58   *Tribute to Vincent Priessnitz inscribed on a stone bath from 'the Temple' to Priessnitz at Ben Rhydding Hydro now removed to the Canker Gardens on The Grove.*

establishment, Priessnitz House, in Malvern (Brooks and Pevsner 2007, 478). Wilson, who also studied with Priessnitz, leased the *Crown Hotel*, Malvern in 1842, renaming it Gräfenberg House (Hembry 1997, 182).

At the peak of the movement in the late 19th century there were over fifty hydropathic establishments in Britain, of which Ben Rhydding was one of the best known, along with Smedley's at Matlock in Derbyshire (Dupree 2007). A somewhat neglected tribute to Vincent Priessnitz can be found carved on a stone bath in the Canker Well garden at the west end of The Grove, now filled with a flower arrangement. The inscription reads 'In Memory of Vincent Priessnitz, the Silesian peasant to whom the world is indebted for the blessing of the system of cure by cold water. This fountain is gratefully erected and inscribed by a grateful Hamer Stansfield. Ben Rhydding.' A well in these gardens came to be known as the Canker Well because of the healing properties the water was thought to have.

Hamer Stansfield, who erected the memorial, was a cloth merchant and the mayor of Leeds. Having benefited from the cold water cure in Gräfenberg, he decided to establish hydrotherapy in Ilkley. He invited Dr Rischanek, who had studied the water cure, to come to Ilkley in 1843 (Constantine 1884, 12) and installed him at Usher's Boarding House in West View, Ilkley, where Rischanek soon built up a flourishing practice for hydrotherapy sessions using the baths at White Wells (Preedy 2006, 54).

In the same year Stansfeld, with four others, bought a large plot of land, previously part of Wheatley Hall Farm (RD OP 523/510) to the east of Ilkley, and formed a syndicate or company to construct a purpose-built hydropathic hotel (RD PC 522/510). The land amounted to 64 acres and included ten acres of Wheatley Woods to the north of the Cow and Calf Rocks. It lay immediately to the east of Ilkley and stretched from

59 *Ben Rhydding Hydro opened in 1844.*

what is now Ben Rhydding Drive to the edge of the golf course. Samuel Sharp, the Leeds architect, was engaged to build the hydropathic establishment, which became the first purpose-built hydro in England. It was located in the southern part of the plot bought by Stansfield, and set at the end of a long driveway leading from Wheatley Lane. It was constructed very rapidly and opened in 1844, having been built in the 'Scottish baronial' style with a central portion, a tower and two wings.

The £10,000 first raised for the building had soon to be doubled, and the final cost was reputed to have been £30,000 including fittings and furnishings. The syndicate was enlarged in 1846 to 27 (RD DXO 130/154), presumably to meet the increased costs of development. Whilst the landowner, Middleton, had agreed to Hamer Stansfield's purchase of the estate at Wheatley there is correspondence between his solicitor and the directors of the Ben Rhydding Hydropathic Company regarding the quantity of stone they were quarrying. Freeholders had 'commonable rights' to gather stone from waste ground for the purposes of reasonable repair and addition to property, but Middleton thought wholesale quarrying of stone for the purpose of building the hydro exceeded this right. He complained that soil and stone was being removed from the raikes, and large quantities of stone and slate were being taken from his moors leading to the creation of large and dangerous holes (Carpenter 1999, 51-2).

The Ben Rhydding Hydro, a very handsome building, was nevertheless completed. On the ground floor was a dining room, library, billiard room and sitting rooms, and on the first floor a drawing room, six private sitting rooms, and four bedrooms all commanding 'exquisite and varied views of the surrounding scenery'. The second floor was devoted to double bedrooms, the south wing to ladies and the north to gentlemen. On each landing was a bathroom and in each bedroom was a bath with an unlimited supply of water direct from the springs. The bathrooms all contained a plunge bath and a douche and there were hot water, hot air and vapour baths, as well as steam apparatus (anon 1858, 13). With a total of 60 bedrooms, the establishment was the first of many hydros built to offer visitors the water cure in Ilkley in the second half of the 19th century. Luxury was combined with the strictest hydrotherapy regime in the country, which involved early rising, careful dieting, and energetic exercise, in addition to the austere hydropathic treatment. This included packing patients tightly in blankets after they had been wrapped in cold wet sheets (Hembry 1997, 173). Ilkley spa water contains no special nutrients but it was cold, pure and soft, and this was sufficient to convince guests of its power to heal (Preedy 2006, 54). Under the hydropathic system, the cure came from the physical effect of the water treatments which were applied in a variety of ways, and not from the effect of any mineral content in the water. Visitors were encouraged to drink two or three pints of water a day and they also bathed in it at near-freezing temperatures. In 1850 a reported 500,000 gallons of moorland water were being piped annually to Ben Rhydding Hydro.

60   *Ben Rhydding Hydro.*

In 1849 the renowned Dr William Macleod of the Edinburgh Royal Public Dispensary was appointed physician at Ben Rhydding Hydro and was also appointed to a post at the Institute for Diseases of Females in Bradford. Macleod gave real impetus to hydrotherapy in Ilkley and continued to develop and extend the Ben Rhydding Hydro. In his medical regime, fresh air was always prescribed along with the water treatments, and good ventilation was contrived in the bedrooms. In 1856 Macleod introduced the compressed air bath and airtight chamber to the west of

61   *Ben Rhydding Hydro.*

62 *Ben Rhydding Hydro, c.1870.*

the house, where moorland air was pumped into a closed room to raise the pressure. The chamber was constructed of iron plates riveted together like those of a steam engine boiler. A covered arcade or gymnasium was added, along with a bowling green, so that medical gymnastics and exercise could be taken in all weathers and by those too infirm to go outside. The grounds were laid out 'to the advantage and pleasure of the patients, affording them the opportunity for varied exercise and communicating also with the

63 *Dr William Macleod of Ben Rhydding Hydro.*

64 *Ben Rhydding Hydro, c.1870 from Hangingstone (the Cow and Calf Rocks).*

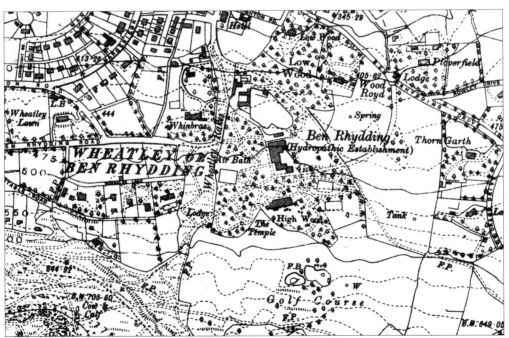

65 *Ben Rhydding Hydro and Grounds, showing the Air Bath to the west of the main Hydro building, the Turkish baths were built in the building to the south near to the Temple which was dedicated to Priessnitz by Hammer Stansfield. Reproduced from the 1906 Ordnance Survey map.*

extensive moors which crown the hills for many miles on both sides of the river Wharfe' (anon 1858, 15, 73).

In 1859 Macleod added a Turkish, or Roman, bath at a cost of £2,000. This new building had three rooms heated to different temperatures. The Frigidarium was 36 feet by 32 foot six inches in area, and 30 feet high, and was floored with coloured encaustic tiles. A decorative fountain surrounded by rocks served as centrepiece. The Tepidarium was a smaller room, octagonal in shape, and around the room were closed recesses with rose-coloured glass in the ceiling. This room was maintained at a temperature between 90 and 110° F, while the hottest room, the Calidarium, was maintained at a temperature between 140 and 150° F. Connected to this room was a suite of apartments called the Wave Douche, the Rain, and other cold water baths.

Macleod relaxed the original regime at Ben Rhydding and in the Turkish Baths adopted Ling's System of Movements, a more gentle Swedish style of massage, as an alternative to the rough Turkish shampooing procedure. The list of available hydropathic treatments was extensive, a wash-down, dripping sheet, shallow bath, sitz, running sitz, sitz douche, head bath, hot water bed bath, wet sheet envelope, eye, finger, foot, knee or leg bath, the spout, rain or needle bath, douche, ascending douche, wet pack, dry pack, compress, spinal wash, spirit lamp, vapour bath, Russian bath, Turkish or Roman bath, or compressed air bath (Wodrow Thomson 1862, 37-56), each treatment designed to be suitable for different ailments. Dr Macleod's development of the establishment is reflected in the description of the estate at the time he purchased it in 1863. In addition to the Hydro building, it included several cottages, a tennis court, hot houses, greenhouses, bathhouses, washhouses, an engine house, a steam engine, boiler sheds, outbuildings yards, gardens and pleasure grounds (RD DXO 130/154).

The accessibility of Ilkley to visitors was improved greatly when the railway line from Leeds and Bradford was opened in 1865. Towards the end of the year the North Eastern Railway Board ordered that 'a small wooden station, with a booking

66 *Recreation room at Ben Rhydding Hydro in the 1890s.*

office, waiting room and retiring room for ladies' be constructed as a temporary measure at Ben Rhydding. Dr Macleod of the *Ben Rhydding Hotel* did not see this as a suitable arrival and departure point for his visitors and patients, however, and reached agreement with the railway board that he would pay for and erect his own stone station building with ornamentation as he saw fit. He owned the station at Ben Rhydding until 1885 when it was sold back to the railway companies for the sum of £240.

The Ben Rhydding Hydro became a popular and well-patronised establishment. It was 'one of the most noted of the hydropathic institutions drawing visitors from all over the world' (Hembry 1997, 173). Records from 1851 indicate a varied patronage; amongst the visitors were a silk merchant from Lancashire, a farmer and a colonial clerk from Scotland, a manufacturer of woollen hosiery from Cheshire, and an undergraduate from the East Indies. In 1862 those meeting in the drawing room at Ben Rhydding were described as 'professional men belonging to different learned professions, merchants, agriculturists, soldiers, sheriffs, Edinburgh writers to the signet, London barristers, solicitors, Episcopalian clergy, English and Scottish dissenters, ministers of the national and free churches, East Indian nabobs ... And among the fairer sex the same variety is seen.' (Wodrow Thomson 1862, 21-2) The most renowned visitor in search of hydropathic treatment was Charles Darwin, who visited the town during 1859 after completing the final draft of *On the Origin of Species*. He stayed in rooms in Wells Terrance and then at Wells House Hydro, where he was treated with cold hip baths by Dr Edmund Smith, and he visited the White Wells Spa. The visit is commemorated in the name of the recently refurbished West View Park, now called Darwin Gardens.

Thomas Carlyle stayed at Ben Rhydding Hydro in 1849. Charlotte Brontë did not stay at any of the hydros, but in 1835 she wrote that she liked the place immensely and made further visits to stay with

67 *Visitors to Ben Rhydding Hydro, c.1860.*

68 *Edmund Smith of Wells House Hydro in 1858.*

believing it had restored him to health and vigour, returned to his home town to practice it, in a milder form but with marked success, among his work people, setting up the Matlock Hydrotherapy Baths (Bulmer 1895, 417).

Hydrotherapy was approved by some of the medical profession and many treatises demonstrating its application to various types of disease were produced. Macleod advocated strongly the idea that hydrotherapy was a system which could maintain and strengthen healthy people as well as treat the sick (Woodrow Thomson 1862, 111). All types of respiratory disease, consumption, diseases of the eye, skin and joints, rheumatism, digestive diseases, female complaints and 'a deficiency of the vital power' were all treated with hydrotherapy. The system seems also to have attracted interest from temperance reformers, who saw in hydropathy a defence against alcohol, and this probably generated even more clients for the water treatment. 'Weakness of the mental faculties' was another ailment thought to be suitable for hydrotherapy (anon 1858, 40), and a hydropathic regime in a beautiful setting was regarded as invaluable for treating mental depression (Wodrow Thomson 1862, 111). An item in the *Ilkley Gazette* in 1882 describes a hydropathic patient who may have been mentally unstable: 'A young woman under treatment at a hydropathic institute at Ilkley a few days ago cut her throat and died.' An unsuccessful attempt was made to avoid an inquest, with 'irritation of the throat' being given as the cause of death. An inquest into the sad case might detract from the reputation of the hydros.

her friend Miss Wooler, who had been her schoolmistress. In 1845 she wrote to her friend Ellen Nussey suggesting an 'excursion to Ilkley' (Smith 1995, 402). She evidently had some faith in the effectiveness of the spa water at Ilkley because in another letter, to her friend Mary Dixon, she was grieved to hear that 'the cold water cure' taken elsewhere had done no good and trusted that the 'air and water of Ilkley' will be more successful (Smith 1995, 336). Satisfied clients of Ben Rhydding also spread the practice of hydrotherapy to other parts of Britain. John Smedley was a hosiery manufacturer at Lea Mills, near Matlock. In 1849 he tried the cold water cure at Ben Rhydding and,

69   *Wells House Hydro opened in 1858.*

The success of Ben Rhydding Hydro led to other similar establishments being built in Ilkley, the most notable probably being Wells House. This was opened in 1856 on the site of a mill, and initially Dr Rischanck was the resident physician (Hembry 1997, 174). Dr Edmund Smith, who stressed his connection with Gräfenberg, Austria, later took over. This was a large three-storied building in Italianate style, planned for one hundred patients and designed by Cuthbert Brodrick, architect of Leeds Town Hall and Scarborough's *Grand Hotel*. In 1856 White Wells was leased to the Wells House Hydro, and it was probably at this time that the bathing areas were roofed and a stable block added to the eastern end of the building. Having improved the White Wells, the company discouraged use of the nearby free bath facility and these fell into disrepair, eventually being converted into public toilets. The Wells House Hydro took a water supply for its own hydropathic treatments from the wells via an underground stone-built water tank which was discovered to the rear of White Wells in 1929.

Around the same time the four-storied 'castellated' Craiglands Hydro, set in grounds of five acres on the hillside leading to the Cow and Calf, opened in 1855. The first proprietors were the Dobson Brothers, Dr Henry Dobson being a physician who supervised all the treatments offered to patients. These included mustard pads, massage, and all the latest Turkish, Russian and Electro-Chemical baths. These systems were

70   *Engraving of Wells House Hydro surrounded by formal gardens.*

71   *Craiglands Hydro.*

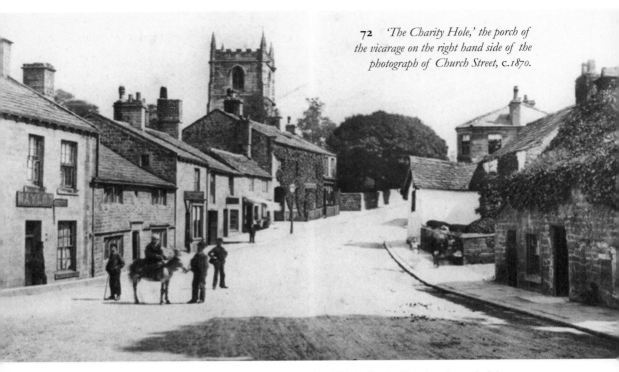

72 *'The Charity Hole,' the porch of the vicarage on the right hand side of the photograph of Church Street, c.1870.*

coupled with the 'tonic' air from the moors. Besides Ben Rhydding, Dr William Macleod also acted as consulting physician at other establishments in Ilkley, his own personal reputation being considerable. At first this was at a small property at Holly Bank, but a larger property constructed in 1859 and intended for those who could not afford the terms at Ben Rhydding, was superintended by Dr Scott, Macleod's junior at Ben Rhydding. Other indications that Macleod was interested in promoting hydrotherapy for all was a reduced tariff at Ben Rhydding for villagers who did not stay at the Hydro (Wodrow Thomson 1862, 106-7). Dr Scott also operated a dispensary for the poor in Ilkley from the porch of the old vicarage (now demolished, once opposite the Manor House, where the entrance to The Arcade now stands). This porch became known as the 'Charity Hole' and it was from here that

the Ilkley Bath Charity, founded by curate George Fenton, also dispensed charity aid of five shillings a week to pay the cost of baths at White Wells for poor invalids. The Bath Charity also founded the first convalescent home in Ilkley in 1829 and in new premises, a large charitable hospital set back from the road on the south side of The Grove opened in 1826. Here, every patient approved by the medical officer was entitled to stay for three weeks, enjoying charitable board, medical attendance and baths; but in the 1900s those wishing to stay longer had to find fees of 7s. a week.

As neighbouring towns grew increasingly industrialised and polluted, Ilkley became renowned as a health resort. It provided an escape and was an increasingly popular resort for visitors as well as being a place where the wealthy settled in large houses built to accommodate families and servants. When the Cowpasture was enclosed in 1858 some building land was released and three further hydros were built, Craiglands in 1859, the Troutbeck Hydro in 1863, and Rockwood House in 1871. In 1883 Stoney Lea Hydro appeared, the proprietor Mr Emmott having been a bathman at Ben Rhydding Hydro (Mellor 1982, 8). All the hotels in Ilkley also developed hydro facilities. Among the first was the *Crescent Hotel*, built by 1879 and owned by 1896 by Miss Jones, a successful employee at Ben Rhydding. Others were the *Middleton Hotel*, *Highfield Hotel* and the *Tarn House Boarding Establishment*. By 1898 another large hydro had been established. The Gothic-style Spa Hydro, originally called The Grove (in 1894), was on the south side of The Grove. Marlborough House was another. As a consequence of all this development, the census of 1891 indicated more domestic servants living in Ilkley than most other West Yorkshire towns.

Hydrotherapy began as a medical regime but the water treatment became less popular and was replaced by the concept of a holiday offering rest and recuperation accompanied by the lure of the romantic landscape and other leisure pursuits. This change, coupled with strong competition from the new hydros, led Ben Rhydding to relax further its regime and introduce other leisure facilities. By 1890 it had archery butts, two hard tennis courts and a large croquet lawn, and boasted the most extensive baths and the grandest recreation hall in the kingdom (Hembry 1997, 174). The true hydropathic regimes may have become less popular but the demand for water

73   *Ilkley Hospital, the new premises built on The Grove in 1862, photographed* c.*1900.*

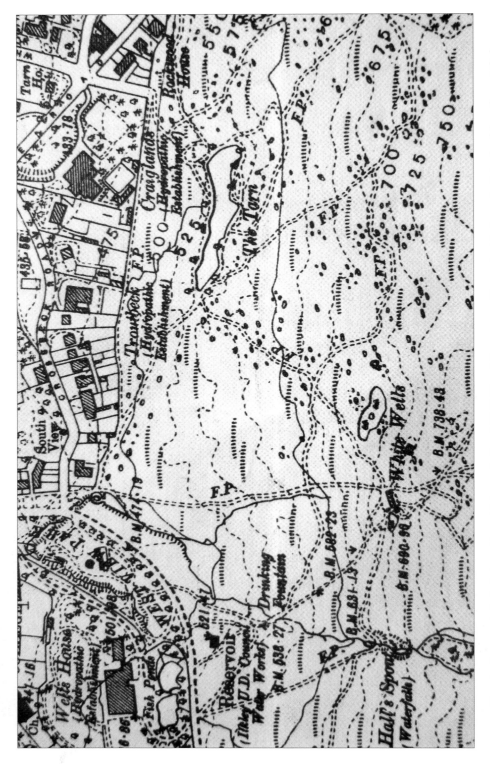

74 Map showing several of the hydropathic establishments built at Mill Ghyll and Cowpasture, with moorland to the south. Reproduced from the 1906 Ordnance Survey map.

75 *Looking down Cowpasture Road from the moor towards some of the hydros in* c.*1870.*

76 *Stoney Lea Hydro.*

77   *The Troutbeck in Crossbeck Road.*

were replaced when the Ben Rhydding Hydropathic Establishment Company was financially restructured and a second company with the same name formed. New Turkish baths were installed and augmented by Russian and plunge baths in a new building connected with the main Hydro. At this time the baths cost 2s. 6d. or 12s. for six, though Bath Blankets and Sheets were provided without additional charge. The staff comprised a Head Bathman, a Head Bathwoman, and a number of supporting bath attendants.

treatments was sufficient for a significant refurbishment to take place. At some time around the early 1890s the original baths

78   *Croquet playing at Wells House Hydro, White Wells Spa on the hillside above.*

Six

THE PLANNED TOWN

The turning point in Ilkley's development did not come until well into the 19th century. Its transformation from a small rural township to a handsome town was in part due to the economic impetus provided by the popularity of its waters and its development as a centre of hydrotherapy, but the coming of the railway and land sales created a period of radical change. At the mid-point of the century the only significant new buildings in the town were the group of hydros in the Cow Pasture and the hugely influential Hydropathic Establishment in Ben Rhydding. In the 1840s the township could still be described as 'a little rustic, inaccessible and primitive place' (Speight 1900, 201), but by the end of the century the experience of visiting the town had been transformed and was described in the following way: 'Today [in

79 *Railway staff photographed in the 1880s at Ilkley Station.*

80 *A photograph taken in the 1900s shows donkeys waiting in line, as a taxi rank, in Brooke Street under the railway bridge carrying the line to Skipton.*

1900] one steps out of the busy station and looks upon the broad and handsome streets with their numerous well built houses, shops and hotels and avenues bordered by beautiful villas, while reaching far along the hill sides are other stately residences and even castle-like hydropathic establishments' (Speight 1900, 201).

The arrival of the railway improved the accessibility of the town and paved the way for the further development. In 1860 the Midland Railway and the North Eastern Railway agreed to build routes linking Ilkley with Bradford and Leeds (opened in 1864-5) and with Skipton (opened in 1888). The increase in the number of residential and day visitors as a consequence is indicated by an estimate of around 200,000

in a year in 1900 (Speight 1900, 220). Some visitors would still have used the roads, and some walked to Ilkley over the moor from Saltaire, Bingley and Keighley

81 *Front page of the sales particulars for one of the land sales at Ilkley.*

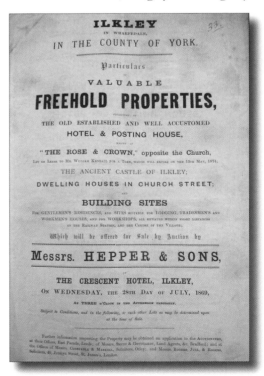

ILKLEY
IN WHARFEDALE,
IN THE COUNTY OF YORK.

Particulars
OF
VALUABLE
FREEHOLD PROPERTIES,
CONSISTING OF
THE OLD ESTABLISHED AND WELL ACCUSTOMED
HOTEL & POSTING HOUSE,
KNOWN AS
"THE ROSE & CROWN," opposite the Church,
LET ON LEASE TO MR. WILLIAM KENDALL FOR A TERM, WHICH WILL EXPIRE ON THE 13TH MAY, 1874;
THE ANCIENT CASTLE OF ILKLEY;
DWELLING HOUSES IN CHURCH STREET;
AND
BUILDING SITES
FOR GENTLEMEN'S RESIDENCES, AND SITES SUITABLE FOR LODGING, TRADESMEN'S AND
WORKMEN'S HOUSES, AND FOR WORKSHOPS, ALL SITUATED WITHIN SHORT DISTANCES
OF THE RAILWAY STATION, AND THE CENTRE OF THE VILLAGE;
Which will be offered for Sale by Auction by
Messrs. HEPPER & SONS,
AT
THE CRESCENT HOTEL, ILKLEY,
ON WEDNESDAY, THE 28TH DAY OF JULY, 1869,
AT THREE O'CLOCK IN THE AFTERNOON PRECISELY.
Subject to Conditions, and in the following, or such other Lots as may be determined upon
at the time of Sale.

Further information respecting the Property may be obtained on application to the AUCTIONEERS,
at their Offices, East Parade, Leeds; of Messrs. SMITH & GREENBANK, Land Agents, &c, Bradford; and at
the Offices of Messrs. CONSTABLE & MARKILL, Solicitors, Otley; and Messrs. ROOKER, JUER, & ROOKER,
Solicitors, 40, Jermyn Street, St. James's, London.

along footpaths which survive today. The arrival of the railway did not detract from the popularity of the traditional mode of transport White Wells. A photograph taken in the 1900s shows a long row of donkeys waiting in line, like a taxi rank, under the railway bridge in Brooke Street.

LAND SALE

The fortunes and misfortunes of the Middleton family played a significant part in how the town was shaped. In the face of significant financial decline, their initial resistance to the coming of the railway softened and land was sold from the estate at Ilkley to the railway companies. However, the predicament of the family worsened and eventually the whole estate at Ilkley was sold. Initially the land was advertised for sale as a whole, in one lot, against the advice of Thomas Constable, Peter Middleton's solicitor, who appreciated that more money might be raised if the estate were sold in a series of lots. Constable also appreciated the value of marketing, recommending George Smith of Bradford to draw up plans that would show 'the wonderful adaptation of the estate for building purposes: showing especially the hills and rocky grounds and woods and waters' (Carpenter 1999, 117). An advert for the estate was placed in the *Leeds Mercury* on 2 June 1866, but the sale was withdrawn because Peter Middleton died the following day. The description of the advertised estate provides a very good encapsulation, albeit of the best aspects, of Ilkley at the time:

> The estates in Ilkley … comprising the magnificent moor, called Rombald's Moor, and the far famed Ilkley Spa Well and baths (supplied by one of the strongest springs of the purest water in the kingdom) and several farms, cottage tenements, woods plantations, wooded glens, accommodation, fields, springs, and streams of water, and building ground to an almost unlimited extent, in situations of unrivalled beauty. The estates, besides the moor land and upwards of 100 acres of woods and plantations, comprises above 800 acres of enclosed land, the whole ranging for a distance of nearly four miles from the wooded banks of the river Wharfe to the rugged cliffs and heathered hills of the moor, at an elevation exceeding 1300 feet. The moor is a first rate breeding ground for grouse, with which it is well stocked. Besides ornamental rocks and crags it contains inexhaustible beds of fine freestone for building purposes and offers indications of other minerals. The freehold of the moor belongs to the Manorial Lords, subject to the commonable rights of the owners of freehold tenancies within the township, the large portion of which will be represented by the enclosed lands now on sale, bringing to the purchaser in the event of enclosure of the moor, beside allotments for manorial rights, a corresponding proportion of the remaining allotments.
>
> The property mainly surrounds the popular watering place of Ilkley and, from the bold and picturesque character of much of the land, offers facilities to an enterprising owner to beautify and develop to an unlimited extent a watering place already attracting, by its splendid and eminently successful hydropathic establishments at Ben Rhydding and Ilkley Wells, by the purity of the air and the beauty of the scenery, crowds of visitors from all parts of the kingdom.
>
> (*Leeds Mercury*, 2 June 1866).

When the estate was put back on the market, land was parcelled into separate lots and sold off in a number of major sales. Five sales over a two-year period between 1867 and 1869 raised £26,000. The Bradford surveyor Joseph Smith was employed to provide plans for new roads and allocate plots of land for various classes of graded building to take place. Some areas were for large imposing houses and villas; in other, separate areas, terraced houses would stand in ranks. The plans involved the preservation of some parts of the old village and demolition of other parts. It seems that Constable and Smith understood that in order to retain and increase the value of land for further sales the town should be developed in a way which would allow for rapid expansion but retain the its attractiveness. The layout of the modern town was crucially set at this time.

In the particulars for the first sale, plots were described as 'valuable freehold villa and other building sites and building properties comprising sites for villas contiguous with the grounds of the Ilkley Wells and Craiglands establishments, and for houses in terraces in Wells Road adjoining the ground of the Ilkley hospital; shops, houses and other buildings; in the centre of town two principal streets in this favoured watering place, and the sites of builders premises, workmen's cottages, adjoining the railway station'. This auction of 44 lots was advertised in the *Leeds Mercury*

82-4 *The pastoral image is retained in two lithographs of views from 'the castle' looking east and west printed in these sales particulars which map out some of the plots for sale in 1869.*

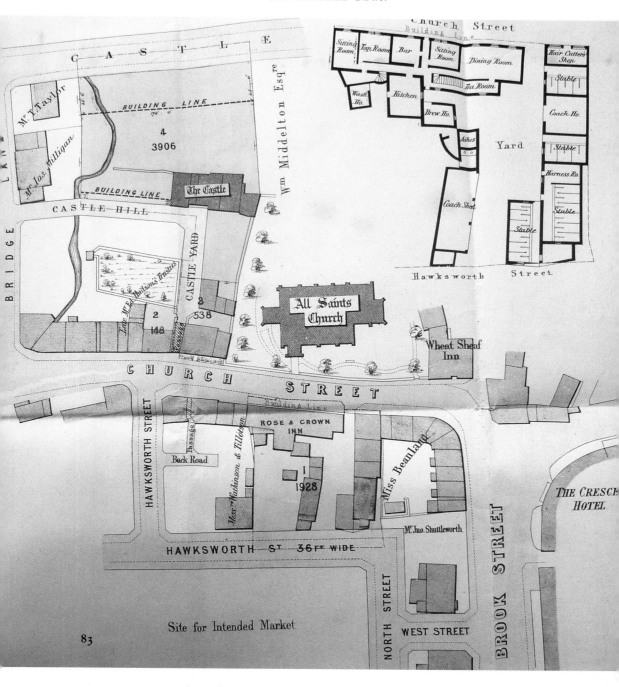

for 11 May 1867 and the highest prices were paid for plots of ground on Brook Street and Church Street close to established shops and dwelling houses. Plots in Wells Road and Green Lane, renamed The Grove, Cowpasture Road and Wellington Road, were also sold, along with plots along the newly planned Craiglands Road.

84

85 *(Above) Inside Hawksworth farm house,* c.*1862.*

86 *Hawksworth Farm House, Hawksworth Street/Brook Street. One of the old farmhouses cleared away after land sales.*

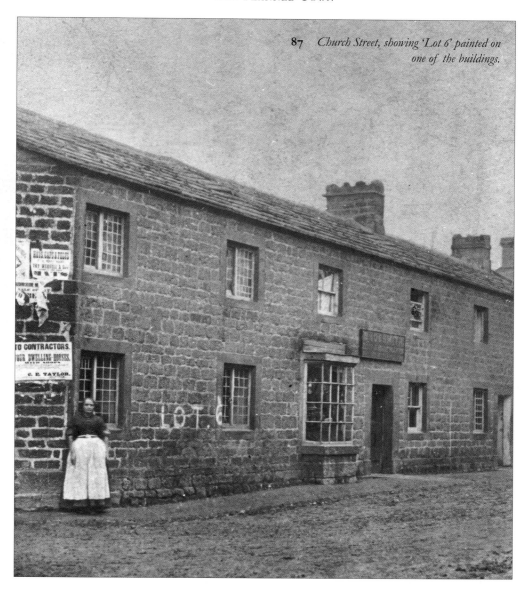

87 *Church Street, showing 'Lot 6' painted on one of the buildings.*

The second sale took place in October 1867 when three fields near to Ben Rhydding, two acres in Ilkley, and some cottages on Wells Road were auctioned. In the third auction in June 1868 building plots adjoining the newly planned roads of Castle Hill, Hawksworth Street, Weston Road, Wharfe View Road, Wells Walk and Ben Rhydding Road were sold. Plots in the centre of the old village were also sold and these included Billy Hawksworth's farm in Brook Street/Hawksworth Street, together with plots on Church Street occupied by old thatched cottages. Buildings appear to have had their lot numbers painted on them prior to auction, a photograph in the Shuttleworth Collection shows a shoesmiths on Church Street, opposite the

88   The Rose and Crown, *Church Street, included in the auction of 1869.*

parish church, with Lot 6 in white paint on the front.

The fourth auction took place in August 1868 and included many building plots on Brook Street, The Grove, Wells Promenade, Railway Road, Wellington Road, Ridings Road, Parish Gill Road, Queen's Road, Princess Road, West Wood Road, Cowpasture Road, Ben Rhydding Road, Wheatly Road, Tivoli Place and Springs Lane. The fifth auction in the following year included the *Rose and Crown* inn, the 'ancient Castle of Ilkley' (now the Manor House Museum), and two houses on Church Street to the right and left of the passageway to the Manor House. By

this time, though, the market appears to have been saturated and many of these plots remained unsold.

CHANGING TOWN AND MOORSCAPE

The plan for how Ilkley would look was encouraged by the conditions placed on the sale of plots. The cost, type of building material, and number of buildings was all specified, very precise suggestions being made for some plots. In the first auction Lot 1 was described as 'a desirable site for a hotel', the plot being where the station hotel now stands. Lots 2 and 5 on the west side of Brook Street were described as 'capital sites for retail shops'. Some lots in the 1869 sale were described as 'most eligible sites for a hotel or tavern', and lots close to the railway station were described as 'eligible for dwelling houses or retail shops'; others on Leeds Road and Lower Wellington Road as 'excellent sites for tradesmen's dwellings'. The town planning made provision not only for new building, but also required the demolition of existing buildings. The conditions of the sale for one plot on the corner of Brook Street and Church Street were that the purchaser should demolish the existing buildings.

The new vision was also very clear and specific as to where any industry would be sited, and that was well away from the new roads where shops and hotels would be. Any 'noisome or offensive trades' were to be carried out in an area at Wellington Road. Planning conditions for plots in this area stated that premises should not be more than three storeys high. No chimney could be higher than 75 feet, and the 'smoke airing shall be effectively consumed by the most modern methods'. Further constraints on the sale of plots stated that 'No slaughter house shall be erected and no noisy, noxious or offensive trade or business shall be carried out in any of the said lots, nor shall the trade or business of

a licensed victualler or beer seller be carried upon any of the lots except 1-4.'

Clear wide roads were a major part of the new town so new streets were laid out and the old ones improved. The Middleton estate was responsible for the construction of roads, sewers and pavements, and the planting of trees and shrubberies, but once established their upkeep was to be a charge on the public rates and the responsibility of the parish, so a Local Board was established to oversee their management. The stream running down Brook Street had been culverted in 1853 but the street was now widened at its junction with Church Street. The demolition of older buildings between 1868 and 1870 produced a change which swept away much of the old village. In 1870 an article entitled 'Progress of Ilkley' and published by the *Ilkley Gazette* marked the huge changes which had taken place in the town, the 'old thatched dwellings, antiquated shops, ugly roads, circuitous sward paths, unlighted streets' having been replaced with 'finer more comfortable dwellings, handsome shops, improved roads and paths, well lighted streets and

89 *(Looking south up) Brook Street after the stream running down the course of the street was culverted but before many shops had been established, c.1870.*

90 *Looking east along Addingham Road to Church Street in the 1860s at thatched cottages with the thatch in a reasonable state of repair.*

91 *A similar view along Addingham Road to Church Street, c.1867, thatched cottages with thatch in poor state of repair.*

92 *Church Street looking east, a penny farthing (invented in 1870s) and other cyclists at the end of the 19th century.*

93   *West side of Brook Street,* c.*1867, before it was re-modelled.*

railway communications' (*Ilkley Gazette,* February 1870). The newspaper argued that the rapid growth of Ilkley could not be attributed to the railway, but rather fawningly said the town was indebted to 'Lord of the Manor Mr Middleton for the opportunity of increasing the bulk and attractiveness of our new town, by

94   *Thatched cottages at the top of Brook Street, opposite the Railway Station before they were demolished.*

the facilities he has afforded, for the purchasing of suitable building sites. This he has done by having land surveyed, some miles of new roads and streets formed and then offering them to the public in suitable lots ... Although it is not three years since the first land was brought into the market, the place has been quite remodelled and the process of development still continues with unabated vigour ... In comparison with other places of resort Ilkley will lack nothing in point of architectural beauty for the buildings ... are greatly varied in design, elegant in form and some of them elaborate in adornment.'

Photographs taken by Shuttleworth, editor of the *Ilkley Gazette*, of the town in the years before the changes and from around 1860 for a 40-year period show the

remarkable and rapid changes which took place after Middleton began to sell land and buildings were constructed on the plots to form the 'new' town.

Many of the initial purchasers of building plots were local people already running businesses in the town. For example, the 'Gothic House' in Brook Street was built on the plot of the Hawksworths' farm by John Shuttleworth. The Gothic House was a fancy goods and stationery shop as well as printing shop for the *Ilkley Gazette* and *Wharfedale Almanac*. Other local purchasers were John Batty, chemist of Ilkley, Thomas Critchley, draper of Ilkley, Elizabeth Beanlands of Ilkley, William Lancaster, farmer with a grocers shop in Church Street, Thomas Lister, owner of the *Midland Hotel*, two of the Dobson

95 *Cottages at the top of Brook Street, c.1866, showing thatched cottages alongside slate roofed houses, includes Lister's refreshment rooms opposite the railway station and a chemist's shop all cleared away for new buildings.*

96 *Lot 1 in the 1869 sale, 'a desirable site for a hotel', the photograph shows the Station Hotel, first named The North View when it was built in the 1870s, with the remains of an old cottage partly demolished next door alongside new shops with awnings for shade.*

97 *Photograph c.1870, re-located from the top of Brook Street, Lister's Tea Rooms in a cottage on the south side of Church Street were the old thatched cottage roof was replaced with slate.*

98   *Photograph, c.1870s. Looking north down a shop-lined Brook Street and at the inns* The Wheatsheaf *and* The Star *at the bottom of the street. These removed when Brook Street extended as New Brook Street in 1891.*

99   *Looking south up Brook Street before the railway bridge carrying the Skipton line was constructed in 1888.*

100 *Looking south up Brook Street after the construction of the railway bridge carrying the Skipton line which opened in 1888.*

family, whose existing interests included *Craiglands Hotel*, and Thomas Robinson, inventor of the invalid couch, builder and joiner. Robinson first had a workshop constructing 'Ilkley Invalid Carriages' in his house on Hangingstone Road but expanded to new premises on the plot at the bottom of Cowpasture Road which he bought at auction in 1868.

His new premises seem to have been the only exception made to the restriction on trades within the designated 'genteel' shopping area. It was a very busy joinery workshop with machinery powered by a steam engine and a smithy. At one time he employed thirty carpenters and he continued in production until 1908 (Smith 2000, 68). The Invalid Coach

101 *Beanlands Grocers' shop on Brook Street.*

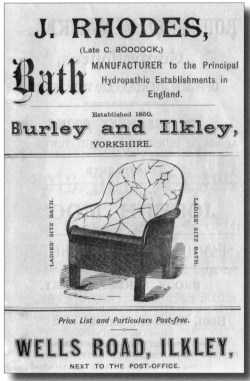

102 *(Opposite, left) Robinson's Invalid Couch constructed in the workshop on Cowpasture Road, advertised in* Shuttleworth's Guide to Ilkley *in the 1890s.*

103 *(Opposite, right) J. Rhodes, a local manufacturer of hydrotherapy equipment advertising the ladies sitz chair in the 1890s.*

104 *(Opposite, bottom) Cycle makers in Ilkley.*

105 *(Right) The Ilkley Brewery also benefited from the Spa town trade, producing bottled spring water.*

106 *(Below) Cottage in Wells Road, one of the lots in the auction of 11 May 1867.*

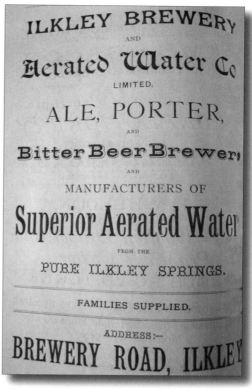

107   *New building constructed at Wells Road on plots sold at auction in 1867 (looking north).*

108   *(The same plots, looking south along West View, Wells Road, with trees planted.*

Works was one among many businesses which developed and flourished locally in order to service visitors to the hydros. In the later 19th century there were at least three chemists in the town, dispensing medicines, tonics and bottled spa water of all kinds to restore the visitors' health. The Ilkley Library Company, a subscription library of 50,000 volumes, thrived on the visitors who made use of its service. John Dymond's livery stables in Wells Road hired horses and carriages to hydro guests for trips to local attractions such as Bolton Abbey, Beamsley Beacon and Harewood House. There were several photography businesses flourishing in the latter part of the 19th century. William Scott and Jesse Bontoft both began with photographer J. Milner and Son, in one of the new villas, West View House, built at Wells Road. They both moved to their own studios; Scotts's in The Grove and Bontoft's in Brook Street, close to Shuttleworth's stationery shop. They all catered to the market for portrait photography and benefited from the trade from visitors to the hydros. Shuttleworth's advert in local guides indicated his willingness to a visit to any hydro establishment at a moment's notice.

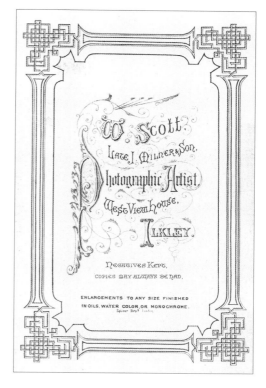

109   *(Above, right) Photographer William Scott, first took over an existing business belonging to J. Milner and Son in one of the new villas, West View House, at Wells Road in 1879 and later, in 1892, moved to purpose-built new premises in The Grove. This advert on the reverse side of a portrait photograph carte de visite shown below.*

110   *(Right) An example of the portraiture photography practiced by William Scott this carte de visite dates from the 1880s.*

As land sales progressed Ilkley expanded. New business premises were built and a middle-class residential population became established in the newly built villas. All the architectural styles popular in the Victorian period were expressed in the new villas which created the suburbs of Ilkley in the latter part of the 19th century and the beginning of the twentieth. The juxtaposition of Gothic Revival, Scottish Baronial, Italianate, Old English Baronial and Arts and Crafts styles has created a variety of responses. The houses described as noble and

111 *(Left) A portrait identified as Mrs Milner of West View House.*

112 *(Below) Jesse Bontoft, photographer advertising in the 1890s (left); Shuttleworth advertising his photography studio in the 1860s (centre); and another Shuttleworth advertisement from the 1890s (right).*

113   *One of the photographs taken by Shuttleworth as a postcard view of Ilkley looking south from the north bank of the river Wharfe, c.1890s.*

114   *One of the photographs taken by Shuttleworth as a postcard view of White Wells.*

115 *Heathcote designed by Lutyens in 1906.*

splendid terraces by the *Ilkley Gazette* were dismissed by Edwin Lutyens as an 'ultra suburban locality over which villas of dreadful kinds and many colours wantonly distribute themselves'. Lutyens himself was responsible for one of the early 20th-century additions to suburban Ilkley. The villa called Heathcote was designed in 1906 and constructed on a four acre site on the south side of Kings Road, fitting between existing plots. The house is in the Italianate style and the gardens were an integral part of the original design,

116 *An advertisement for one of the many new schools in Ilkley Wharfedale School in the 1890s.*

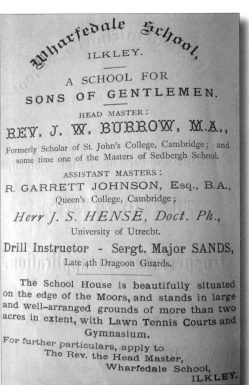

Wharfedale School,
ILKLEY.

A SCHOOL FOR
SONS OF GENTLEMEN.

HEAD MASTER:
REV. J. W. BURROW, M.A.,
Formerly Scholar of St. John's College, Cambridge; and some time one of the Masters of Sedbergh School.

ASSISTANT MASTERS:
R. GARRETT JOHNSON, Esq., B.A.,
Queen's College, Cambridge;

Herr J. S. HENSÈ, Doct. Ph.,
University of Utrecht.

Drill Instructor - Sergt. Major SANDS,
Late 4th Dragoon Guards.

The School House is beautifully situated on the edge of the Moors, and stands in large and well-arranged grounds of more than two acres in extent, with Lawn Tennis Courts and Gymnasium.
For further particulars, apply to
The Rev. the Head Master,
Wharfedale School,
ILKLEY.

Gertrude Jekyll being responsible for the planting scheme (NMR).

The growth of the town and its population resulted in the need for more churches, schools and public buildings. An extended parish church, All Saints, was no longer large enough and the new larger St Margaret's was built in 1874-5 at Queens Road, designed by Norman Shaw. At the beginning of the 20th century the ancient parish was also divided, a separate parish being established for Ben Rhydding (Le Patourel 1968, 27). A Friends Meeting House was built on Queen's Road in 1869. Methodists worshipped in a meeting house in a workshop to the rear of Brook Street until a church was built on Leeds Road (now demolished). A National school was opened in 1872 in Leeds Road, replacing the Old Grammar school. There were several small private establishments, including a girls boarding school in Bilberry Bank, and Crossbeck House, both on Crossbeck Road, another in Mount Pleasant, and several day schools. Ilkley College in Queens Road was first opened in 1869, and in the same year a boy's high school was opened on Parish Ghyll Road but it was closed in the 1880s. In 1893 the new grammar school was opened, and the *Ilkley Gazette*, reporting the scheme for the school approved by the Charity Commissioners, said it was 'to be a day and boarding school, and accommodation to be provided for not less than 100 scholars. The tuition fees were to be at the rate of not less than £5 nor more than £12 a year for any boy.'

New educational trends were also reflected and a Frobelian school opened in 1896 in The Grove opposite the Spa Hydro, with Miss Mildred F. Field, graduate of Newham College, Cambridge, as principal.

117   *A classroom in the Froebelian School, opened in The Grove in 1896, opposite the Spa Hydro.*

118   *John Shuttleworth printer and editor of the* Ilkley Gazette *and owner of new shop premises at the 'Gothic House' in Brook Street built 1869 on the plot formerly occupied by Hawksworth's farm.*

119 *The town of Ilkley as it had developed at the turn of the century. Reproduced from the 1906 Ordnance Survey map.*

120 *A fallen boundary marker on Ilkley Moor, inscribed 'ILB', Ilkley Local Board.*

The growing town also needed a new system of administration and in 1865 a Local Board was set up, but it was unsuccessful and was dissolved. In 1869 a new Board was elected, its political complexion a mixed one, but it was led by Dr Macleod of Ben Rhydding Hydro, a Liberal. Internal arguments amongst board members and with the Middleton estate meant progress was quite slow. The rival influences of Middleton and Macleod were reflected in the newspapers of the time. In 1871 Macleod set up his own newspaper, the *Ilkley Guardian*, in competition with the *Ilkley Gazette*, whose proprietor John Shuttleworth was an ally of Middleton. Conflict between Middleton and the Local Board arose partly over who should pay for maintenance and partly

121 *The Tarn when first created from the former Mill race and pond, 1873-4.*

from the different outlooks of the two political parties. Middleton was particularly resistant to change where he felt it would affect his sporting moorland interests, whereas the Board was keen to administer a burgeoning new town.

Ilkley Moor was the cause of several disputes between the Local Board and Middleton. Ancient rights of common included the collection of stone for building repair, grazing rights and the right to dig turf. Middleton attempted to prevent any interference with the moor, complaining even when visitors walked across it. But the moorland was an essential part of the town's attraction to visitors, walking and exercise in the fresh air being an important part of 'the cure' for those attending first the spa and then the hydros. Guidebooks

emphasised the attraction and beauty of the moorland countryside. In 1876 William Constable, Middleton's solicitor, made unsuccessful attempts to arrange a compromise whereby the Local Board would be able to improve the lower part of the moor out of the rates, but the higher part would remain 'a more quiet preserve for game [while] the lower part improve in beauty and convenience for the benefit of the town' (Carpenter 1999, 147).

Despite these differences, work was carried out on the lower moor to create additional attractions for visitors. In 1873-4 the mill race and pond above Mill Ghyll was enlarged to create The Tarn and this became a long-standing attraction. It provided an attractive skating rink when frozen over.

122 *Skating on the frozen Tarn.*

123 *Skating on the Tarn, c.1954.*

Further attractions were created in 1887 when the Local Board leased from Marmaduke Middleton a plot of land above the wood at Heber's Ghyll and laid out footpaths to provide scenic access to a new chalybeate spring at Heber's Ghyll. In 1892-3 Middleton sold the freehold of this property to the Board along with the manorial rights, along with the mineral, water and sporting rights to Ilkley Moor including Hollin Hall Moor, Silver Well Farm, the Panorama Rocks, the Allotments and part of Heber's Ghyll Wood. Some 1,560 acres of this was common land and the remainder freehold. The Board agreed

124 *Hebers Ghyll in the 1880s.*

to pay £13,500 over a term of 50 years from money raised from the rents of the White Wells, quarries, shooting and grazing rights on the land. The sale of this land established public right of access to around 2,000 acres of moorland and woodland and has played an important part in retaining the attraction of Ilkley to visitors through the 20th and into the 21st century.

RESORT TOWN: ILKLEY 'HEATHER HEALTH SPA'

There were signs of decline in hydropathic establishments in the 1880s due to an over-provision of hotel and hydro facilities and the declining popularity of water treatments. In a very competitive market some hotels had to make reductions in their charges. During the following decade, however, the town consolidated and continued its planned expansion. In 1892 the Local Board described Ilkley as follows: 'Ilkley is, in point of fact, a brand new town – not perhaps of mushroom growth exactly; but it is within the last forty years or so that the place has assumed its present aspect and that celebrity as a health resort has become known far and wide' (1892, 4). The development of Brook Street had been taken a further stage in 1891

125 *The construction of the New Bridge taking New Brook Street across the Wharfe, 1904.*

126 *Green Lane cottages demolished the old lane replaced by the pavements of The Grove in the 1890s.*

when seven and a half acres were bought in the town's centre and New Brook Street was extended to the river, where a new bridge was built in 1904. Two old inns at the bottom of Brook Street were demolished and a new hotel was built there.

One of the main streets in Ilkley, The Grove (once Green Lane), was planned as a promenade in the 1890s and its wide pavements provided a perfect place to promenade, with quality shops providing genteel relaxation and refreshment for visitors. In 1891 the farm buildings and the rustic Green Lane cottage were demolished. Shops catering for the leisure activities of visitors were established over time, and included artist supplies, booksellers, milliners, needlework supplies, photography shops and a piano showroom. Genteel cafes were another feature, the

127   *The Grove looking west with canopies covering the wide pavement in front of the shops, 1890s.*

128 *Looking south at the junction of Brook Street and The Grove.*

129 *The Grove, corner with Brook Street looking west,* c.*1900.*

130 *The Grove, looking east, c.1916.*

Grand Café, the Imperial, the Kiosk and the Spa all setting up on The Grove. At the end of the decade the shops at the western end of The Grove were added, a canopy covering the pavement in front of them being supported by a delicate filigree of ironwork. Several banks were built at this time and grouped at the corner of The Grove and Brook Street. Close to the new home of the Bradford Old Bank was Shepherd, a chemists in Brook Street, which advertised itself as the sole proprietor of

131 *Sapwells and Co. Ladies' Hosiery, gloves, laces, aprons, berlin wools and fancy goods, one of the shops on the north side of The Grove 1892.*

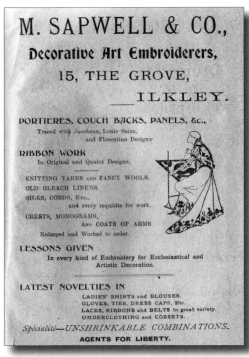

M. SAPWELL & CO.,

Decorative Art Embroiderers,

15, THE GROVE,

ILKLEY.

PORTIERES, COUCH BACKS, PANELS, &c.,
Traced with Jacobean, Louis-Seize,
and Florentine Designs.

RIBBON WORK
In Original and Quaint Designs.

KNITTING YARNS and FANCY WOOLS.
OLD BLEACH LINENS.
SILKS, CORDS, Etc.,
and every requisite for work.

CRESTS, MONOGRAMS,
And COATS OF ARMS
Enlarged and Worked to order.

LESSONS GIVEN
In every kind of Embroidery for Ecclesiastical and
Artistic Decoration.

LATEST NOVELTIES IN
LADIES' SHIRTS and BLOUSES.
GLOVES, TIES, DRESS CAPS, Etc.
LACES, RIBBONS and BELTS in great variety.
UNDERCLOTHING and CORSETS.

Spécialité—UNSHRINKABLE COMBINATIONS.

AGENTS FOR LIBERTY.

the perfume 'Ilkley Moor Breeze', and described 'this elegant preparation' as 'a delicate and lasting fragrance particularly agreeable and refined'. It was sold in bottles with a representation of the Cow and Calf rocks on the label (Guide 1892, 27).

An illustrated guide to the town produced by the Local Board in 1892 shows the character of the shops on the main streets at the time: 'Nowhere are the improvements which have combined to render Ilkley a

132 *(Left) Sapwell and Co. The Grove advertising in the 1900s.*

133 *(Below) William Scott, photographer's studio opened on the south side of The Grove in 1892.*

134 *The Grove, looking east, 1950s.*

135 *Advertising the annual visit of the circus, an elephant walking down Church Street with a train of interested children, c.1899.*

136   *Royal Magnets travelling players at the Bridge Pleasure Gardens, 1900s.*

fashionable and much frequented inland watering place more apparent than in the many fine shops which have sprung up to meet the requirements of the numerous visitors to this highly favoured health resort. The Brook Street of less than a century ago was but a village road with a stream running down its centre, quite rural and almost deserted in its lonely simplicity; whilst today it is a comparatively busy commercial centre, containing a goodly number of well-stocked shops' (Guide 1892, 26). In the Edwardian period it was evident that a host of attractions continued to bring visitors to Ilkley. Pleasure gardens were developed near the bridge by the river. By 1900 Septimus Wray had established the formal attraction of the Pleasure Gardens, where boats to take out on the river could be hired and where swings and other attractions included a band for dancing on Saturdays. Travelling theatre players provided entertainment at the Bridge Pleasure Gardens.

Formal Gardens were laid out at West View and a new bandstand was opened here in 1904.

137   *Formal gardens at West View Park in 1900s.*

138 *West View Gardens and bandstand, c.1904.*

139 *Musicians at the bandstand 1900s.*

140 *Excursions were advertised from Ilkley to Bolton Abbey and other beauty spots, these had once used carriages for transport but the char-a-banc became the mode in the early 20th century.*

141   *The new civic buildings, town hall and library.*

In 1908 Station Road became the site of the purpose-built civic centre, town hall and free library. This range of buildings was designed by William Bakewell of Leeds and cost £13,000, Andrew Carnegie giving £3,000 for the library. The buildings included a museum and the King's Hall theatre. In 1915 a Winter Garden, an essential new attraction for a resort town, was added to the newly built public offices.

142   *The laying of the foundation stone of the library building.*

143   *The opening ceremony at the new Town Hall, April 1908.*

With the First World War came a serious slump in trade for the hydros and hotels, although a book for injured soldiers did recommend Ilkley as a good place to stay for those whose treatment included rest and occasional baths (noting, though, that it was best to stay in the summer) (Fortescue Fox *et al* 1917, 50). Some visitors still visited for their health, and in the early 1920s Ben Rhydding Hydro was still advertising its attractions in the Official Town Guide: 'a full set of baths and Russian baths, three new hard tennis courts, a croquet court and a putting green'. Stoney Lea and Craiglands still advertised as hydros in the same guide, but Wells House was now describing itself as a hotel. Wells House had croquet lawns and in 1923 extended its attractions by building tennis courts in the grounds (YAS 83D89/2/28).

The reason for staying in Ilkley had changed gradually. The hydrotherapy treatment was replaced by the general idea that Ilkley was a healthy place to visit, and the town remained a holiday resort, serving what was essentially a luxury market. The spa credentials continued into the 20th century, when Ilkley advertised itself as 'The Heather Spa'. An advert for the *Ben Rhydding Hotel* in a local guide of the 1930s pointed to the benefits of the location and possibility of health through exercise, describing itself as a golf hotel rather than one supplying hydrotherapeutic treatment: 'The highest and largest hotel in Wharfedale, 600 feet above sea level. Excellent cuisine, central heating, passenger lift, electric light, garage for 50 cars, golf and tennis (3 hard courts) free to visitors, squash rackets, 77 acres of garden and grounds adjoining the open moors. Ideal

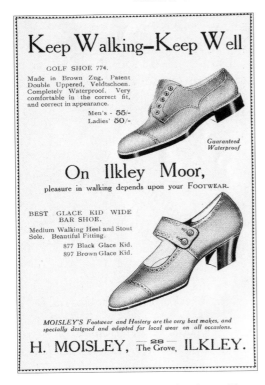

144 *An advert for Moisley's shoe shop on The Grove catering for the needs of the golfer and walker in the 1920s.*

for a restful or a strenuous holiday or as a permanent residence.'

In 1931 Wells House Hydro traded at a loss of £543 4s. 5d., indicating a slump in trade, but the *Ilkley Gazette* reported in 1932 'There is every indication that Ilkley will enjoy a record Christmas so far as the number of visitors to the hydros and hotels is concerned. The popularity of spending the Christmas season in this manner is obviously increasing and very many of the Ilkley establishments have been booked up since the end of November. The Ben Rhydding Golf Hotel said, "If we had as many rooms again we could fill them. We are absolutely full and are refusing about ten a day."' A steady flow of visitors came into the town during holiday periods by bus, train and on foot from the surrounding industrial towns. The bathing pool at White Wells, the river and the moors were all great attractions. White Wells Baths continued in use under the management of the Local Board. Feeling

145 *Postcard of the White Wells with refreshment pavilion.*

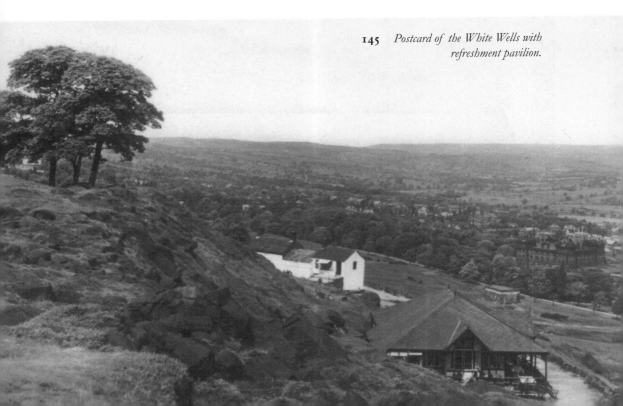

the need to enhance its attractions, the Board initially envisaged a promenade being developed along the ridge where White Wells stood (1892, 4). A 'refreshment pavilion' was built here at the beginning of the 19th century, but this has since been demolished, although its foundations can still be seen to the east of White Wells. Refreshments were an important aspect of Ilkley's attraction and a soda fountain and ice cream parlour at 26 Brooke Street was added to the many more genteel cafés in the town in the early 1920s.

Although the emphasis had always been on taking the spa waters, swimming in the river has long been popular in the summer months. In 1881 the *Ilkley Gazette* reported that there had been several meetings of residents 'with the aim of forming a swimming club and it appeared at that time that the forming of a club would need the sanction of the Lord of the Manor and his views on the matter had been requested. If a club could be formed it would put an

end to the regular and exposed bathing which has been practiced for many years at that part of the river above the bridge called "the Sandbeds", against which complaints had been received by nearby residents. It is the express intention of the club to bathe only at early hours and to wear university costume and to have a suitable tent for changing.' A number of schemes for swimming baths were put forward and in May 1935, the year of the Silver Jubilee of King George V, the Ilkley Lido opened. A cafe at the lido was opened later the same year. The pool has an unusual shape, being similar in plan to the cross-section of a sliced mushroom, the circular portion being 46 metres in diameter. The very fact the pool is not square adds to its architectural interest and rarity, and it also has a rare example of a still unscreened fountain. Dressing rooms were provided for men and women on opposite sides of the pool, although

146 *A postcard of the lido in the 1940s.*

147   *The Lido,* c.*1954.*

148   *The lido,* c.*1960s.*

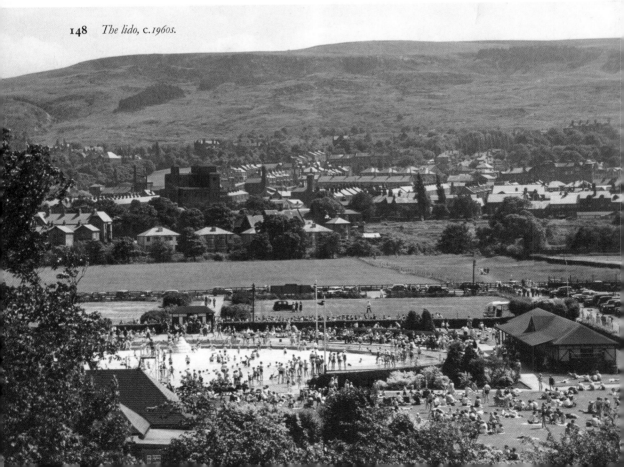

149 *The lido, 2007.*

these were replaced by facilities inside the adjacent indoor pool which was built later. The lido still opens from May to September each year, attracting up to 150,000 visits. Swimming in cold water, in the open air, at this architectural gem, with spectacular moorland views, is an experience which evokes historical connections with the spa waters which first made Ilkley famous.

The hydros and hotels suffered during the Second World War, Craiglands being the only one to open to the public during that time, the others being taken over by government departments. Wells House and a large part of Ben Rhydding Hydro were used during the years 1935-42 to house the Wool Secretariat which offered employment to local people. The town

became a 'reception' area for evacuees partly on account of its ability to accommodate large numbers of visitors (Brown 2006, 92). After the war the Ben Rhydding Hydro stood empty for a number of years and was finally demolished in 1955. Today none of the hydros retain their original function, and the stone gate piers at the end of the drive to Ben Rhydding Hydro are all that remain of this imposing building in its extensive grounds.

Some of the other large hydros have been demolished, Stoney Lea on Cowpasture Road being replaced with a block of flats in 1981. The Sermon Convalescent Home on the edge of the moor was also demolished. However, many of the other establishments have been converted into flats, convalescent

150   *Stone gate piers at the former entrance to the now demolished Ben Rhydding Hydro.*

151   *Wells House Hydro, became the College of Housecraft and later was converted into apartments.*

152 *The remaining plunging pool at White Wells.*

homes, hotels or schools. These include the Spa Hydro, originally called the Grove Spa, at the western end of The Grove, which has been turned into residential flats and shops. Rockwood in Cowpasture Road is now flats and the Toutbeck is a nursing home. Modern housing has infilled the area where the town meets the moor and where large building plots were once occupied by single buildings. The imposing architecture of Wells House survives, becoming the Ilkley Homecraft College until, more recently, it was converted into flats. The White Wells spa was allowed to become derelict but was restored in 1972 and it is still a significant landmark on the moor above the town. One of its two baths remains open and a 'certificate of plunging' into the cold waters can be obtained on completion of the effort.

Bibliography

Anon (A Graduate of Edinburgh University), 1858, *Ben Rhydding The Principles of Hydrotherapy and the compressed-air bath* (London)

Anon (M), 1813, *Wharfedale or a description of the several delightful features of the extensive and splendid valley* (W. Walker, Otley)

Bailey, B., 1852, *Ilkley, Bolton Abbey and The Pearls of Craven* (Bingley)

Bailey, R., 1996, *England's Earliest Sculptors* (Toronto)

Bogg, E., 1904, *Higher Wharfedale*

Boughey, K.J.S. and Vickerman, E.A., 2003, *Prehistoric Rock Art of the West Riding* (West Yorkshire Archaeological Service)

Bradley, J., Dupree, M. and Durie, A., 1997, 'Taking the Water-Cure: The Hydropathic Movement in Scotland, 1840-1910', Welcome Unit for the History of Medicine and Department of Economic and Social History the University of Glasgow, *Business and Economic History*, Vol.26

Brooks, A. and Pevsner, N., 2007, *Worcestershire* (Yale University Press)

Brown, C., 2006, *Images of England, Ilkley at War* (Tempus, Stroud)

Brown, R., 1793, *A General View of the Agriculture of West Yorkshire* (Edinburgh)

Bulmer, T. and Co., 1895, *History, Topography and Directory Derbyshire*

Carpenter, D., 1986, *Ilkley, The Victorian Era* (Smith Settle, Otley)

Carpenter, D., 1999, *The Road to Ruin, The Lords of Ilkley Manor, The Middletons of Stockeld 1763-1947* (Smith Settle, Otley)

Charlesworth, D., 1969, 'Ilkley Roman Fort; Iron Age settlements and field systems; Aldborough Roman site', *Archaeological Journal*, Vol. 125

Cockshott, A., 2008, *Ilkley King's Hall 1908-2008* (Bradford Metropolitan Council)

Codrington, T., 1919, *Roman Roads of Britain*

Collyer, R. and Horsfall Turner, J., 1885, *Ilkley Ancient and Modern* (Otley)

Colton C., 1835. *Four Years in Great Britain 1831-1835*, Vol. II (Harpers, New York)

Constantine, J., 1884, *Hydrotherapy at Home: The Domestic Practice of Hydrotherapy*

Cooper, W. (ed.), 1927, *Ilkley Parish Registers*

Cowling, E.T., 1946, *Rombalds Way A Prehistory of Mid-Wharfedale* (William Walker, Otley)

Cowling, E.T., 1969, 'The Cornmills of Mid Wharfedale' (Otley Archaeological and Historical Society)

Cramp, R., James, T., 2002, 'Corpus of Stone Sculpture in North Yorkshire' (British Academy)

Dixon, M., 2002, *Ilkley, History and Guide* (Tempus, Stroud)

Dodson, M., 1971, 'Ben Rhydding, Hydropathic Establishment' (Leeds College of Education thesis)

Drake, F., 1736, *Eboracum, The History of York*

Dupree, M., 2007, 'Varieties of Practice and the Curative Power of Water: Unqualified Hydropathists in Nineteenth-Century Scotland' ('Water and Health in the Nineteenth and Twentieth Centuries', Venice)

Elgee, F., 1930, *Early Man in North East Yorkshire* (Gloucester)

Forshaw C.F. (ed.), 1907, *Yorkshire Notes and Queries*, Vol. III (Bradford)

Fortescue Fox, R., Tait MacKenzie, R., Hernaman-Johnson, F. and Beaver Mennell, J., 1917, *Physical Remedies for Disabled Soldiers*

Granville, A.B., 1841, *The Spas of England and Principal Bathing Places* (Henry Coburn, London)

Haigh, D., 1988, 'Ribchester to Ilkley: Roman Road,' *YAS Roman Antiquities*, Winter 1987-8

Hagerty, J., 1992, *Myddelton Lodge: A Brief Historical Guide*

Hartley, B.R., 1966, 'The Roman Fort at Ilkley', *Proceedings of the Leeds Philosophical and Literary Society*, Vol. 12 part II

Hartley, B.R., 1987, *Roman Ilkley* (Olicana Museum and Historical Society)

Hembry, P., 1997, *British Spas from 1815 to the Present, A Social History* (edited and completed by L. and E. Cowie, The Athlone Press, London)

Ilkley Archaeology Group Bulletin, 1955, nos 1-12

Ingle, G., 1997, *The Yorkshire Cotton Industry 1780-1835* (Preston)

JHC, *Journal of the House of Commons*, Vol. 7, 1651-1660, pp.156-7

Langdale, T., 1822, *A Topographical Dictionary of Yorkshire* (2nd edition, Northallerton)

Leyland, J., *Leyland's Itinery* (the Yorkshire portion, complied by Thomas Bradshaw reprinted by *Yorkshire Archaeological Journal*)

Le Patourel, J., 1968, *Ilkley Parish Church* (2nd edition, Gloucester)

Long, M., 2005, *Ilkley in 1847* (Mid-Wharfedale Local History Research Group, Ilkley)

Luke, T.D., 1919, *British Spas and Health Resorts of the British Isles* (A.C. Black, London)

Mellor, E. (ed.), 1982, *Images of Ilkley in the 19th and 20th Centuries* (Bradford Metropolitan Council)

NMR, National Monument Record, *National Archives*

Norton Dickon, J., 1898, *Bradford Antiquary*, Vol. III

Olicana Historical Society, 1976, *Ilkley Remembered* (Otley)

Page, W. (ed.), 1912, *A History of the County Yorkshire*, Vol. 2 (Victoria County History)

Page, W. (ed.), 1935, *A History of the County of Rutland*, Vol. 2 (Victoria County History)

Paterson, D., 1795, *A New and Accurate Description of all the Direct and Principal Cross Roads in Great Britain* (London)

Pickles, M.F., 2002, *Pre-Victorian Ilkley, 1672-1811* (Mid-Wharfedale Local History Research Group, Ilkley)

Pigot, 1829, *Directory*

Pigot, 1834, *Directory*

Preedy, R., 2006, *Ilkley, Town and City Memories* (Francis Frith Collection, Salisbury)

Purdy, J.D., 1991, *Yorkshire Hearth Tax Returns* (Hull)

RD, references documents held by West Yorkshire Record Services (Sheepscar, Leeds; Bradford and Wakefield)

Rivet, A.L.F. and Smith, C., 1962, *The Place Names of Roman Britain*

Romilly Allen, J., 1884, 'The Crosses at Ilkley', *Journal of the British Archaeological Association*

Romilly Allen, J., 1879, 'The prehistoric rock sculptures of Ilkley', *Journal of the British Archaeological Association*

Ross, P., 1913, 'The first stage of the Roman Road from Ribchester to York', *Bradford Antiquary*

Taylor, H.M., 1969, 'Ilkley Saxon crosses; Otley crosses; Ledsham church; Kirk Hammerton church', *Archaeological Journal*, Vol. 125

Shaw, T., 1830, *History of Wharfedale* (William Walker, Otley)

Short, T., 1734, *Natural, Experimental and Medicinal History of the Mineral Waters of Derbyshire, Lincolnshire and Yorkshire*

Smith, M., 1995, *The Letters of Charlotte Brontë* (Oxford University Press)

Smith, R., 2000, 'The Rise of the Gentle Suburb, Ilkley 1850-1891' (MA thesis University of Leeds)

Smedley, J., 1864, *Practical Hydrotherapy* (London)

Speight, H., 1900, *Upper Wharfedale: Being a Complete Account of the History, Antiquities and Scenery* (London, reprinted 1988, Smith, Settle)

Stone, L., 1990, *Road to Divorce: England 1530-1987* (Oxford University Press)

Vyner, B., 2008, 'The Neolithic, Bronze Age and Iron Age in West Yorkshire Research Adgenda' (West Yorkshire Archaeological Service)

Warburton, J., 1720, Map of Yorkshire

Waterton, C. (ed. Irwin, R.A.), 1955, *The letters of Charles Waterton*

Wardell, J., 1881, *Historical Notices of Ilkley, Rombald's Moor and Baildon Common* (Leeds, first published in 1869)

Weaver, L., 1925, 'Houses and Gardens by Edwin Lutyens', *Country Life*

Whitaker, J., 1773, *The History of Manchester* (Manchester)

Whitaker, T.D., 1878, *History and Antiquites of the Deanery of Craven* (3rd edition, Leeds, reprinted 1973; first published 1812)

Wodrow Thomson, R., 1862, *Ben Rhydding: the Asclepia of England* (Ilkley)

Woodward., A.M., 1920, 'A Decorative Bronze Silenus-Mask from Ilkley', *The Journal of Roman Studies*, Vol. 10, pp.185-8

Woodward, A.M., 1926, 'The Roman Fort at Ilkley', *Yorkshire Archaeological Journal*, 28

WYAS, West Yorkshire Archaeological Service

YAS, references documents held by Yorkshire Archaeological Society

ILKLEY LOCAL STUDIES LIBRARY

Ilkley Gazette

Photograph collection, 1860s to early 20th century

LOCAL GUIDES

1829, *A Visitor's Guide to the Beauties of Ilkley* (Knaresborough)

n.d. (*c.*1884), *The Sixpenny Ilkley Guide Book and Directory* (Lund and Co., Ilkley)

Bailey, B., 1852, *Ilkley Bolton Abbey and the Pearls of Craven* (Bingley)

Denton's, 1871, *Ilkley Directory and Guide Book* (Ilkley)

Denton's, 1884, *Ilkley Directory and Guide Book* (Ilkley)

Ilkley Local Board, 1892, *Ilkley in Wharfedale Illustrated Guide* (London)

Ilkley Urban District Council, 1911, *Ilkley Guide* (Ilkley)

Ilkley Urban District Council, n.d (before 1915), *Ilkley Official Guide* (Ilkley)

The Ilkley Development Council, n.d (*c.*1920), *The Offical Guide to Ilkley and Ben Rhydding, The Heather Spa* (Ilkley)

The Ilkley Development Council, 1922, *The Offical Guide to Ilkley and Ben Rhydding, The Heather Spa* (Ilkley)

Ilkley and Ben Rhydding Publicity Association, *c.*1937, *Ilkley and Ben Rhydding, the Heather Spa*

Ilkley Urban District Council, 1954, *The Official Guide to Ilkley* (William Walker, Otley)

Ilkley Urban District Council, 1956, *Heather Spa Official Guide to Ilkley* (William Walker, Otley)

Shuttleworth J., n.d (1864), *Guide to Ilkley*, 2nd edition (Ilkley)

Shuttleworth J., n.d (after 1882), *Guide to Ilkley*, 3rd edition (Ilkley)

Shuttleworth J., n.d, *Guide to Ilkley*, 5th edition (Ilkley)

Shuttleworth J., n.d (after 1900), *Guide to Ilkley and Vicinity*, 8th edition (Ilkley)

Index

Numbers in **bold** refer to illustrations.

The town of Ilkley as it had developed at the turn of the century. Reproduced from the 1906 Ordnance Survey map.